# DARK PERSUASION

Ultimate Guide on Persuasion, Manipulation, and Body Language Skills. Learn How to Mastering NLP Techniques and Mind Control Methods to Change People's Behaviour
(2022 Crash Course)

## Theobold Lee

1

# TABLE OF CONTENTS

4

# INTRODUCTION

Dark psychology is the study of a person's state. It includes the psychological nature of people who prey on others with a motive for the crime and deviant behavior, as well as crime and abnormal behavior lack goals and instinctual attraction.

General assumptions about the theory and all people can harm other people and creatures Although many people limited or sublimated this trend, some people took measures against these impulses. Dark psychology attempts to understand the systems of thoughts, feelings, perceptions, and personal processing that lead to predatory behavior in contrast to the modern understanding of

Dark psychology assumes that crime, delinquency, and abusive behavior are all for a reason, and that 99.99 per cent of the time, they have some intellectual, persistent motivation. This is the remaining 0.01 per cent of the dark part of dler's theory and teleology's psychology.

Dark psychology suggests that there is an area in the human mind that allows some people to commit violent behaviour without purpose. This is referred to as a dark singularity in this theory. Dark psychology believes that humanity ha an evil intent to consciously relate to others, from minimal, ambiguous, and fleeting thoughts to purely psychopathic deviant behavior. This is referred to as the a dark continuum. The confounding factor is called dark psychology. A softening factor is an accelerator or attractant next to a mysterious singularity. Outrageous human behaviour falls on a dark channel.

The following is a brief introduction to these concepts. Dark psychology is a concept that has struggled for fifteen years, and he recently comprehended the philosophy, psychology, and determination of the state of man " Dark psychology is not only the dark side of our moon but also the sum of all satellites' dark sides." " Dark psychology encompasses all those who connect us to the dark side. This well-known cancer exists in all cultures, beliefs, and people. We all have a hidden side within us from the moment we are born to die; some call it evil, while others call it crime, pervert, and painful. Dark Psychology introduces a third philosophical concept, arguing that this behaviour differs from religious teachings and modern social science theories " This is a person who is uninterested in his country. The greatest challenge in their lives is the greatest harm to others. This person is responsible for a person's failure. "Dark Psychology" believes that some people will behave in the same way, not for the sake of power, money, gender, retaliation, or any other known reason. They committed this terrible acts aimlessly.

Simply put, their result does not justify their means. Some people infringe and cause harm to others. In the research field, we all have the potential to harm others without cause, explanation, or purpose. Dark psychology believes that this dark potential is very complex and even more dark to determine. Dark psychology suggests that we all have the potential for a predator's behaviour and that it can penetrate our thoughts, feelings, and perceptions. As you can see from the text, we all have this potential, but only a few of us act on it. We've all had thoughts and feelings about cruelty. We fantasize about hurting others cruelly and mercilessly.

However, if you are honest with yourself, you will have to agree with the thoughts and feelings you had about committing heinous behaviour. Given this fact, we consider ourselves to be the right kind. I want to believe that we believe that these thoughts and feelings do not exist. Unfortunately, we all have these ideas, and luckily, no action was taken against them. Dark psychology consists of the fact that some people have the same thoughts, feelings, and opinions as others, but they manifest their influence unintentionally or impulsively.

The apparent difference is that they act on themselves, whereas others have only short-term thoughts and feelings about it. Dark Psychology believes that this predator's style is purposeful and has rational, persistent motivation. Religion, philosophy, psychology, and other dogmas have all made compelling attempts to define dark psychology.

Most human actions associated with evil acts are truly purposeful and purposeful, but dark psychology believes that purposeful actions and purposeful motives seem blurred in the field.

There is no apparent rationality or pure mental perversion from thought to pure mental perversion, and dark psychology has suffered several injuries. The dark continuum helps to comprehend the philosophy of dark psychology. Dark psychology affects that part of human psychology or the general condition of a person that allows and may even contribute to predatory behavior.

Some characteristics of this behavioural trend lack obvious rational motivation, versatility, and predictability in many cases. Dark psychology believes that this general human condition is distinct or a continuation of evolution. But let's take a look at any of the basic development principles. First and foremost, remember that we evolved from other animals. We are now the standard for all animal life. Our frontal lobe gives us supreme beings.

Let us assume that the summit's creature does not completely remove us from animal instinct and predatory nature. "The stronger you experience a sense of inferiority, the stronger the desire to win, and the more intense your emotions." Assuming you believe in evolution, which you do, you believe that all behaviours are associated with three basic instincts. The three main motivations for humans are sexuality, aggressiveness, and selfsutaining instincts.

Progression adheres to the survival principle of the most adapted and breeding species. We and all other forms of life can reproduce and survive. Ggression is to designate our territory, protect our area, and ultimately gain reproductive rights. This sounds reasonable, but it is no longer a part of the human condition. The warmth of our thoughts and perceptions makes us the culmination of both types and cruel practices. And if you've ever seen a nature documentary, you'll undoubtedly be shaken and saddened by an antelope torn apart by the pride of a lion. While cruel and regrettable, the purpose of violence is consistent with the evolutionary model of selfdefense. Lions kill the food they require to survive. Male animals occasionally die in battle for territorial ceremonies or the power of the will. "De sees that people always persecute others, but always they were persecuted." When animals hunt, they usually go after and kill the youngest and weakest women in the group.

Although this reality may appear a little psychotic, the reason for choosing prey is to reduce the likelihood of injury or death. All animals live to act in this manner. All of their cruel, violent, and bloody actions are linked to evolution, natural selection, survival, and reproductive instincts. You will discover this after reading this manuscript, and there is no "dark psychology" application for the rest of the planet. We are people with what dark psychology is attempting to explore. When we study the human condition, it appears that the theories of evolution, natural selection, animal instinct, and their theoretical principles and their theoretical principles and their theoretical principles and their theoretical principles So, we're the only creatures on the planet that hunt each other, and there's no reason for this species to reproduce. Humans are the only creatures that hunt other creatures for unexplainable reasons. Dark psychology believes inner psychology that influences our actions and is anti-evolutionary.

We are the only species that kill each other for reasons other than survival, food, territory, or breeding. For centuries, philosophers and churchmen have tryed to explain this phenomenon. We'll delve deeper into some of huan malice's historic explanations.

Only we humans have apparent rational motivation to harm others.

Dark psychology assumes that some people are human becaue we are human, and we promote dark and vicious behaviour. As you may have guessed, this place or field is shared by all of us. No group of people has a dark side now, before, or in the future. Dark psychology believes that this type of human condition lacks rationality and logical rationality. And this is a part of all of us, with no known explanation. Dark psychology holds that this dark side is also unpredictable. It is impossible to predict who will act on these dangerous impulses.

However, the feeling of kindness toward some people is ultimately denied, and its length will be even more unpredictable. Someone has raped, killed, tortured, and violated people for no reason. This behaviour has been demonstrated by dark psychology. They act as predators in huan prey search wthout a clearly defined goal. As humans, we are putting ourselves and all other beings in grave danger. There are numerous reasons, and dark psychology attempts to investigate these risk factors. The more readers can imagine dark psychology, the better prepared they will be, and the less likely they will fall prey to human predators. And before continuing, it's essential to have a mere understanding of dark psychology.

When you finish the future manuscript, this structure will be expanded, and the most important concepts will be presented in detail.

# CHAPTER 1

# WHAT IS MANIPULATION?

## What exactly is manipulation?

Manipulation is simply the use of calculated techniques to try and change how things are today for your benefit. It is non-physical and can be used in a negative way to cause damage, such as stealing, or in a positive way to avoid danger, such as rescuing. That being said, the manipulator's needs, and the victim's strong will, govern its power. When compared to someone who always completes what they set out to do, a person who is naturally forceful wields a greater degree of power. However, this is not an excuse for manipulation because, in reality, everyone has a choice about whether or not to give in to their urges.

**Psychology manipulation**

The definition of control varies depending on who is doing the characterizing. It is characterized frequently as the demonstration of getting somebody to do or say something through astute and handy impacting with respect to the controller. Few definitions even venture to show the absolute most observable characteristics and examples of mental control that must be available in a person's conduct with their Mental, enthusiastic, and mental mutilation to deal with contemplations and activities Conditional and individual abuse (or exploiting any shortcoming or opening they discover in an individual or circumstance)

Regardless of who you are conversing with and their involvement in control and control procedures, most individuals associate the word with negative activities and now and then pitiless techniques for an impact that causes torment to This perspective is exact now and again, and anybody can perceive any reason why, can perceive any reason why can perceive any reason why. It is a direct result of how dull and perilous manipulative individuals have demonstrated to be looking back when encounters are examined, and individuals attempt to recapture control of their lives

All things considered, control (in human brain research) is a method for overseeing another person accomplish a specific objective without them getting aware of any outside influence or compulsion.


## Difference Manipulation or Persuasion?

The distinction between control and influence lies at their very center and the contents that make them what they are. As we learned in the previous section, influence is the way toward changing somebody's convictions, considerations, or emotions to get their help or get them to make a specific move. The definitions sound nearly identical, so how would you tell the difference between influence and control when various strategies are recognizable and being used around you? Influence and control can now and then be befuddled as a similar idea or two of a kind. At their center, influence and control are two totally extraordinary mental strategies that can be ued for both constructive and adverse outcomes, depending on the individual using them and how Influence is one strategy that can be used to empower someone into making a move that they were opposed to or against from the start. This is regularly done by giving somebody realities about the circumstance being referred to, for example, reminding your companion they need to work in the first part of the day when it begins to get

Control, then, is a progression of methods and strategies shaped into a deliberately spread out arrangement to get somebody (or a gathering of individuals) to change their musings, sentiments, or Control meanings frequently include words like shrewd and capable, alluding to the insidious, corrupt, and crafty nature of the individuals who practice this type of Dark Psychology.

**What exactly is covert manipulation?**

Clandestine Manipulation, similar to Covert Persuasion, is regularly characterized as the strategies and systems controllers utilize that can't be distinguished or even perc few people take up control as their calling, regularly winding up in criminal or mentally harming (to themselves as well as other people) attempts that

**What exactly is dark manipulation?**

Dim Manipulation takes the obscure and regularly wicked thought processes of general and clandestine control procedures and maxes them with different strategies, hypotheses and parts of D

It tends to be hard to see the diference (here and there unthinkable, depending on the methods ued and the ability of the person at ung them to control others) a

**A Master Manipulator's Characteristics:**

The most ideal approach to have the option of shielding yourself from being the objective of control is to realize how to detect a Master Manipulator before they find the opportunity to make you simply one more Most manipulative individuals lean toward unpretentious and determined methodology. These individuals frequently exhibit symptoms of psychopathy, sociopathy, and narcissism. It is another, but similarly malignant gathering of Master Manipulators who grasp progressively forceful (once in a while brutal) control systems that are anything but difficult to spot when experienced The dreadful truth is that, regardless of which type of Master Manipulator individuals end up facing, when most control unfortunate casualties understand that something isn't right, it is past the point where it is possible

One of a Master Manipulator's most outstanding qualities is their capacity to structure and hole up behind mental covers to win individuals' trust or make some shared view for an apparently more profound

Mental covers regularly begin to shape dure adolescence and other significant changes in life when individuals begin to adjust parts of their character (purposely or By adulthood, the vast majority are beginning to passionate development, mental dependability, and adjusted social aptitudes and capacities xcept if the individual has purposefully shaped a mental cover to wear as a method of controlling others.

Here is a more intensive glance at several of the more well known Personality Personality Personality Persona Masks concluded and worn by those considering the specialty of control:

The Pleaser of People: People Pleasers base their primary assessment of themselves on how others see, depict, and feel about them. Rather than voicing their own suppositions around others, they tune in and concur with the prevalent attitudes shared by everyone around them, so they generally have companions and strong associations paying little h

Controllers make this to the following stride and put their People pleaser cover on to agree with everybody they converse with, particularly if they need the individual they're prevailing on to accomplish This can be a perilous strategy for controllers with  It turns out to be considerably more hazardous when the individuals around them are different and dwell on the furthest edges of the range with regards to picking their sides on some On the off chance that the controller agrees with one individual and, at that point, is heard concurring with another person of the contrary conclusion, they've recently caught themselves in a circumstance where

Hero Mask: This is a more straightforward and secure veil than controllers wear. Individuals who wear this cover need to feel like the saint or the person who is required in some random circumstance and is normal in the expert world. In any case, controllers thrive on having others do things for them, so the ones who additionally have a courage complex (and can deal with the two effectively) have built up their techniques for being viewed The advantage of this is that they can fill jobs that are gainful to how others see them and their property when an objective is met or an undertaking is done successfully.

This type of cover can likewise be flipped by experienced controllers wear the Hero veil when conditions are certain and occasions play out the manner in which they Because of the human component of the circumstance (through and through freedom, defects, and passionate reactions), there is always a chance that a control method will reverse discharge, regardless of how well it was When this happens, the accomplished controller knows to flip their Hero veil to uncover the opposite side of its inclination, the Martyr cover. This side of the cover paints the wearer as the unfortunate casualty so as to feel sorry for and occupy consideration from their job throughout occasions or as an approach to reduce the seriousness of For controllers, this side of the veil has been planned not exclusively to gain feeling sorry for yet to totally move duty regarding the failures on the individual they were They assume the fault; the controller is given another opportunity or excused dependent on their absence of command over the activities of the other individual (most definitely) and the controller has recently added another helpful experience to their general information and practice of Dark Manipulation using Psychological Personality covers.

Because of their requirement for control, the individuals named controllers will mentally incline toward their own organization or make a gathering of individuals around them that have lower certainty or are increasingly thoughtful. This implies that finding a group of manipulative individuals cooperating is unusual. Another explanation behind this is Master Manipulators are regularly worried about their own advantage and advancement, paying little mind to the damage Controllers will be attracted to authority positions in general becaue they have an ability for getting individuals to do whatever they are advised or welcome to participate.

# CHAPTER 2

# RECOGNIZING MANIPULATORS

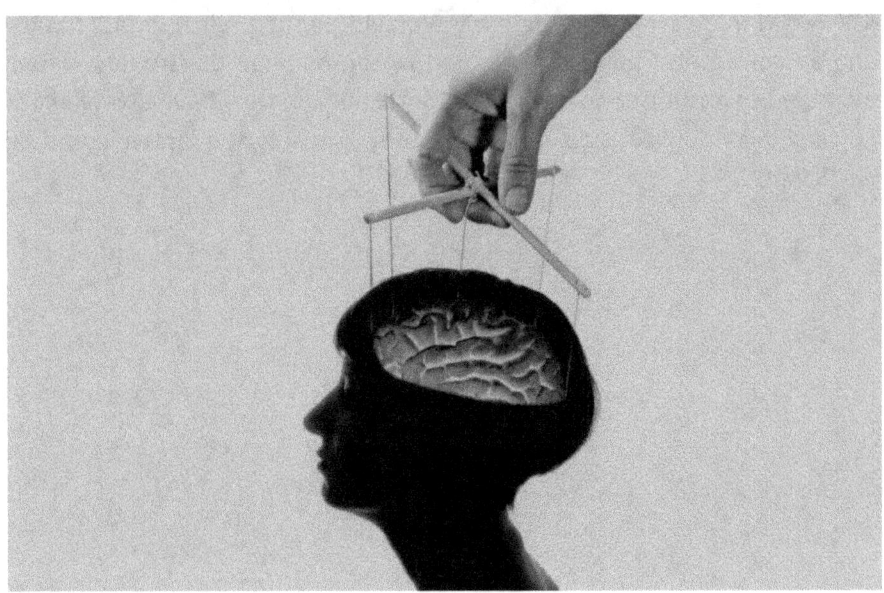

**Golden Key**

Someone has an impact on each of us. Sometimes someone's opinion is important; sometimes it's the attitude; sometimes it's the wishes — head, wife, lover, friend, a famous magazine, public opinion in the person of "unt Tasha," the cleaning lady.

If you can identify people whose opinions are important to your future interlocutor, consider that you have already practically prepared the ground for negotiations—unless, of course, you can influence them.

And when they tell him ten times from different sources how wonderful you are, how good it is to deal with you, how important it is to listen to your opinion and go towards you, you just have to appear and voice your proposal.

**Become a mythical person**

Experienced negotiators collect all available information about the other side. So, make certain that all available information about you plays on you. Make a myth about yourself out of rumours, gossip, stories, and legends! And make t available to the masses Furthermore, the reputation, of course, has not been canceled.

Allow your opponents to obtain contradictory, sometimes erroneous, and mysterious information about you. Or they just gain the belief that you need to be friends, taken care of, cared for, and cherished.


**Arouse your emotions!**

In a conversation, if you control emotions, you control enough. You may have gaps in your argument and stretch your logic. You may not have any rationale at all. If only it were up to you what the interlocutor would go through.

The ability to arouse intrest, delight, joy, pleasure, curiosity, attraction, fear, doubt, insecurity, anger, and disgust—this is all that is required for negotiation success. If that is the case, the first will follow.

If the interlocutor does not see the logic in your words but likes your ideas, he will invent them himself. If the opposing party does not agree with your arguments but feels sad and regretful at the same time, he will be able to persuade himself. You will succeed if you can control your emotions.

The interlocutor's local local local local local local local loca

It became clear that the creators were sitting here in the morning, the light of the indescribable stupidity that the brain always emanates, exhausted by hours of brainstorming -

**Anonymous.**

It can also have an impact. Directly and indirectly, If you consider negotiations for your interlocutor's deadline and he simply does not have time to look for other options, his condition is beneficial to you. Especially if you pull the time politely. If he "accidentally" poured mud over his car this morning, he will not be pleased. If they called him during a meeting with you and told him the good news, he will be more generous. If he holds a cup of roasting coffee poured to the top, her attention will be riveted.

Biorhythms, health, "random" meetings, background music, lack of sleep, day of the week—all of thee and more affect the physical and psychological state of the interlocutor. And if you think about how to use all of this, you can "make" yourself the best negotiator.


**Pain points, weaknesses, fears, and uncertainties**

"Sir," a student wondered, "how did you find out she loves nuggets so much?"

"Learn how to ue the Internet, Daria," I explained. - Fool in the "interests" is writen everywhere in plain text.

Ny friends, old and new, information about the psych type, obervation of behavior and reacts—any strength has a dual weakness. We examine. We are looking for optimal exposure methods—because it would be incorrect to use this information headon. Only leave as a last resort.


**Play weaknesses**

Most people, regrettably, are cars. In the sense that they live quite mechanically. There is a stimulus, and there will be a reaction. You get the result by pressing the button. Lready on this alone, you can build

It is now critical for us that when you click on some buttons, people completely automatically give out stormy experiences. It is necessary to yell at someone, threaten another, praise the third, admire the fourth, show the fifth to the sixth, show the "sex-friendly" object, take the seventh away—of course, different As a result, if the interlocutor did not respond meaningfully to one provocation, you should move on to another.

To do so, you must first understand the list of basic human weaknesses. For example, there are these:

- Superiority
- Greed
- Pity
- Sex
- Patriotism
- Masculinity
- Femininity
- Fear
- Wine
- Generosity
- Envy
- Jealousy
- Justice
- "Weak?"

Over time, you will learn to determent what that person will do by eye. You can just do a bust in the meantime. Alternatively, switch to another way to set your interlocutor off balance for your antics to work.


**We are not robots, and robots are not us.**

Information collection is standard. We're looking for patterns along the lines of, "In the situation 'X,' he acts 'U.'" accordingly, we can provoke the "U" we need by crafting the corresponding "X." For instance, when they praise his car, he blurs with a happy smile. What needs to be done to make him smile? If he only agrees to the third proposal, the first two cannot be soared. The third step is to make it profitable for us.

On the other hand, if we know which external signs are responsible for which internal reactions, we can "read the thoughts" of the interlocutor, which is convenient. Take a look for patterns!


**Development of territory**

They claim that special forces differ from ordinary well-physically and psychologically trained troops only in one way: the completeness and quality of information about the enemy and the location of the future massacre A model of the future theater of operations is built up up up up up up up up up up up up up up up up up u Then, tactical combat schemes are planned and practiced by being automatic. As a result, special forces and can destroy superior enemy many times, and even on its territory.

If the information is false, the special forces are doomed. And no hand-to-hand combat with mark shooting aids them—foreign territory.

The irony is that many people attend important "meetings" with them despite not having mastered their own territory. You should still propose to master what truly fits into any framework.

The best alternative to negotiation - Remember, Daria: the manager's authority is based not on what he said, but what he doed. Daria, learn to send! Learn to decide whether or not to send it! This is a crucial skill. Everyone will use you until you master it—you do not master the profession until you master it. And you, on the other hand, should use them all!

What will happen if negotiations fail? What are you going to do? Whom should I contact? Simply put, if your alternatives are the sea, you are calm, like a boa constrictor, and can easily take risks and play on the verge of a foul. And the attitude ares—that game. If you have a lot of options, you will not put up with the inconvenience. If you don't have a choice, you'll have to come to terms. If you have nothing to fear, you will not employ harsh and unappealing methods. People who have pressed against the wall are capable of any meanness.

Search for alternatives! Extend your selection! Investigate the market. Make an offer to many. And when the cost of defeat falls, there will be significantly more victories.


**Allow the walls to assist you:**

"Perhaps I shouldn't go to the palace?"

- Walk here! Sorrel raised his voice. "i'll need a henchman."

- henchman, henchman, henchman, henchm

- Well, yes. The very first degree of apprenticeship is the only one who listens to me — err, cast spells — and admires them.

It's great when it's up to us where we'll meet with the interlocutor! After all, we can make everything play for us. Or a great deal. The ideal situation is when you have fully developed the territory but it is completely unfamiliar to him. Then you've almost won.

If everyone around you respects you, the interlocutor will inevitably respect you. It is also good if the music helps to create the right mood sounds. You have an advantage if it depends on you what will be served on the table. If everything that happens unintentionally distracts his attention, and you are used to it, everything is just wondrously wondrously wondrously wondrously wondrously wondrously wondrously wondrously wondrously wondrously wondrously wondrously wondrously wondrously

Certain people's appearance and disappearance. Calls for mobile. Shine. Music. Furniture. Make a temperate atmophere! Also, don't forget about your convenience. If you need quick reference information, let convenient access to the Internet be nearby. The territory is a well-knit affair.

**Who's there?**

If your support group is nearby, with an approving hum that meets all of your remarks, and is ready to boo any creep in your direction, the opponent will be difficult.

In any case, regardless of who is nearby, it is sometimes more useful to influence the interlocutor through the audience. Very often, speakers do not turn to the opposition, who will object at any time, but to the public, which will support it sooner. Allow your words and actions to beautifully beautifully beautifully beautifully beau Attractive. And well if he himself is apprehensive about his actions. Witnesses determine!

As a result, inviting rude negotiators with their wives—for a dinner party, for example—can be useful. Then they automatically lose all the advantages of the usual style of communication—against the background of a man who, in theory, should have played on her side.

Everything is clear here: we make the maximum margin of time for ourselves and adjust to the maximum margin of time for the other side. Then we are calm, and time plays with us. And the opposing twitches Because time is working against him.

**Where is the world going?**

Where are oil prices going? What is the state of the labour market? Where does the political chain go? What major competitors will enter the market soon? And if you know what market is, you can guess what political, cultural, etc. Situations will play on you at some point.

**Laws, exceptions, customs, and rules**

Win-Win Lawyers live by this: they find the rules confirming the clients' correctness. And the fact that a good lawyer can find arguments in favor of almost any side clearly demonstrates that you need to know the laws.

It is beneficial to be aware of your legal rights. It is beneficial to be aware of the responsibilities of others. To ensure that you comply with the law. Or, at the very least, what you require right now.


## Master the territory

The described approaches to preparing for negotiations may suggest that the meaning of any negotiation is to squeeze the opponent dry. This is not correct. I still believe that leaving behind grateful people is preferable to leaving behind offended ones. It is more ueful for buness— and for health.

# CHAPTER 3

# THE DARK TRIAD

Abusers frequently fall into this category—the dark triad. The dreaded three personality types that combine to create a human storm capable of destroying lives so utterly that the individuals have little hopee of reassembling them without intensive professional These personality types are dark—they do not care about people and encompass everything wrong and toxic about humanity. They are frequently monsters within human skin, staring out into the world and wreaking as much havoc as they can as quickly as possible. These three traits, Machiavellianism, narcissism, and psychopathy, are dangerous enough on their own, but be warned—you are better of leaving when you still can and

# Machiavellianism

"The means justify the ends." This phrase came from the text he wrote in The Prince in 1513— he informed the prince that was being instructed within the document to present himself in one way, honest The message, is essentially summarized by saying that the ends justify the means, meaning that it was acceptable to lie because it make the prince more well-liked, and a well-liked leader

Based on that principle, Machiavellian people are adept at appearing the way thoe around them want them to see them. They will say whatever those around them want to hear because they know it is unlikely that those around them will ever know the truth, and telling them what they want to hear makes them happier and gets the Machiavellian.

The result, then, justifies the means of lying, even though lying is typically considered morally wrong and reprehensible.

This personality type is quite insidious—you never know if what you are seeing is what you are getting. Machiavellian (Machiavellian = Machiavellia

The individual is deceitful and a master at deceiving those around him or her. They will only tell the truth if it is beneficial to them or the most desired outcome, which it is not in most cases. They believe that it is more important to seem desirable and make good connections than it is to develop actual proper relationships with people, but if you see people as nothing more than a means to an end, you are unlikely to ever

When people are nothing but means, they have been dehumanized, turned into nothing more than tools to be used to get what you want in any way possible simply because you want that result. Finally, despite the immorality of the behaviour, you will do whatever it is that you must to get the result you want simply because it will get you what you want and that is all you really care about at the end of the day.

These people should never be trusted—they always have an ulterior motive, no matter how honest they appear at the moment. There is always something motivating them to behave in certain ways, whether it is innocent or not is debatable. You would be better off avoiding and not trusting this person whenever possible.

## Narcissism

The narcissist is the second member of the dark triad—individuals with narcissism suffer from a narcissistic personality disorder. This is characterized when an individual presents with a grandiose sense of self, meaning he is quite egotistical and believes that he actually is, a pervasive la The narcissist thrives on having his or her sense of self-justification validated through actions such as praise or admiration—they only see themselves as worthwhile if others around them see them as worthwhile first. They want to be recognized as worthy and will go to any length to achieve that.

This means that narcissists are frequently willing to lie about who they are or what they like—they have no true sense of themselves beyond someone that desperately seeks the approval and admiration

The narcissist typically creates an alter ego, a persona that he presents to the world that is everything he wishes he were— charismatic, powerful, influential, and well-liked. He then ues several dark psychology manipulation techniques to keep people under the spell he seeks to create. He creates a sense of himself and then constantly plays mind games and manipulates those around him. Only those who get close enough to him to be ensnared in his web of lies beyond hope of getting out ever see his true self—the malicious individual that lies beneath the persona, lurking for the first possible chance to lash

After capturing a victim in his trap, he will systematically manipulate the other person, conditioning them to do whatever the narcissist desires. Over time, he can shape his victim into the ideal source of constant admiration; something referred to as his narcissistic supply. He will then use manipulation and mind control techniques to keep his new toy under his thumb for as long as possible, attempting to systematically break down his victim by any means necessary.

# Psychopathy

Psychopaths suffer from their personality disorders, which are frequently characterized by a series of persistent antisocial actions. They almost always lake an real sense of empathy—the innate human ability to connect emotionally with others at any meaningful level. This lack of empathy makes them extremely dangerous. Without empathy, which is a built-in red flag system that lets us understand when something is wrong with those around us, particularly in regards to our behaviors to others, the psychopath has no re For those who do feel empathy, the pain they, themselves, feel as they harm someone else, I usually enough to make them stop. The pain and guilt become overwhelming, and they stop before making matters worse. The psychopath, on the other hand, does not believe that.

Aside from a lack of empathy and thus remorse, psychopaths typically exhibit disinhibited behaviour—in other words, they are impulsive. Their mind will pop into their mind with some random impulse, such as stealing a purse from someone or deciding to hurt another person, and they are far more likely upon it simply because they like to act upon their impulses.

Psychopaths are frequently bold—they do not really fear anything they are approached with. Consequences are not frightening. People are not frightened. Even dying or being harmed does not frighten the psychopath. The psychopath is extremely tolerant of danger and is frequently observed to have high levels of confidence and assertiveness, even though he is unlikely to want to do anything meaningful with that confidence—he sees no point in engaging in social convenience.

With the three personality types now described in an easy-t0-understand manner, you may be wondering what happens when the three are combined. The result is an aggressive, toxic individual who does not care to act in a normal manner. They are fantastic at exploitation, lacking the empathy necessary to impede such negative, harmful behavior, and having the right amount of lack of impulse control to encourage it. They manipulate, they hurt, they lie, and they steal. They are callous, which means they do not care about the feelings of others and revel in seeing people who are hurt, angry, or sad. According to research, people with the dark triad personality type enjoyed seeing people with negative expressions on their faces.

Finally, those possessing the dark triad are not forces to be reckoned with—they will do anything to hurt you if you wrong them, and they do not care enough about social conventions to be held back from seriously harming you.

# CHAPTER 4

# MANIPULATIVE TECHNIQUES

Manipulators employ a variety of techniques to gain complete or partial control of their victims: Manipulators are frequently on the lookout for personality types to prey on. The reason for this is that they feel the need to easily manipulate their victims. They look for vulnerable parts in others and use them against them.

Most of the time, their prey is nave, empathetic, those with low self-esteem, or lacking in confidence. The following are some standard techniques ued by manipulators:

**Gaslighting**

It is a type of manipulation that employs three distinct phrases: "it didn't happen," "you're insane," and "it's your imagination."

31

Some experts believe that this is one of the most dangerous manipulative techniques available, as it aims to disorganize and kill the victim's sense of reality.

When a person is manipulated by this technique, he loses touch with reality and can no longer trust himself. Worse, the victims of this type of manipulative technique do not feel the need to call the manipulator for maltreating them.

## Projection

In this type of manipulation, the manipulator looks for someone else to blame for everything that goes wrong around them. It is something that most people have, but it is more common among narcissists and psychopaths.

The manipulator employs a defense tactic, which entails shifting responsibility for wrongdoings and negative attitudes and blames everything on another person aside from himself.

## Generalizations

It happens in cases where a person chooses to misunderstand another intentionally for ulterior motives.

Have you ever found yourself in a situation where a sibling, for example, refuses to consider the long-term consequences of his or her parents' actions? Though you haven't said anything, this sibling informs everyone who cares about listen that you called your parents "wicked" simply because you stated that you were not comfortable with a certain major decision they are making for you.

In situations like this, you wonder what is going on and begin to believe that your sibling did not understand what you said. The truth is that this type of person clearly understands their victims, but they choose to run with an entirely different story.

It is widespread with narcissists who are not very good at making sound intellectual decisions because they are plain lazy. When it comes to their brains, they would rather make a hasty generalization of whatever a person says than make a critical assessment of another person's word.

They frequently draw conclusions and make statements that are not consistent with the thoughts and words of their victims, and they do not try to look at things from a different perspective to see where their victim is coming from or consider the reasons; they said what they said.

**Relocating the goalposts**

Moving the goalposts is a common logical fallacy, and sociopaths and abusive narcissists make fair use of it all the time. In this case, the manipulator ensures that they always have a cause to complain about their victims, not because they are not pleased with their victims' actions or words.

Even in cases where the victim has found every possible reason to justify their actions, validate their words, or even do things to meet their demand, they remain adamantly dissatisfied. In most cases, they simply raise their expectations or change their terms, or they simply request that you provide more proof.

**Changing the subject**

It may appear to be a harmless action, but it is not. Manipulators use techniques such as changing subjects in conversations. This is a way to avoid being held accountable for their words or actions.

It is also familiar with narcissists because they do not want to ever dwell on a topic that requires them to be responsible for anything. To avoid this, they simply find ways to change issues in their favour. This type of manipulation will continue for as long as the victim allows it to happen. It becomes difficult to have relevant discussions in situations like this. Whenever the manipulator is present.

**Name-calling**

It is a technique that entails attacking the victim's personality by calling him derogatory names. Most victims may believe this is normal because they have become accustomed to it from bullies in school to parents, friends, or partners who call them names, but it is not, and it is just as destructive as other manipulative techniques. This type of manipulation can be found in all aspects of life, including presidential politics.

**Devaluation**

It is shared with friends or colleagues who tend to show love to you while always having bad or terrible things to say about the last person in your place. This is something that narcissistic abusers always do.

When it comes to intimate relationships, they have very terrible things to say about their exes. Still, the new partner will eventually determine why the ex was such a "terrible partner" becaue the narcissist will ultimately mate the same treatmen This person can be found in a professional setting just as much as it can be found in a personal setting.

**Making aggressive jokes**

Sometimes you find yourself uncomfortably amused by someone else's jokes. Your sense of humour may not be the problem, as you will be led to believe. Perhaps the main problem is the motive behind the joke.

Some people take pleasure in making malicious comments at the expense of others. These comments may be presented as jokes so that they can easily pull it off without consequences. This way, they can say terrible things without having to apologize for them.

Because they keep their innocence in saying what they want to say, you are rendered powerless and unable to complain because anytime you try to react, you are seen as one who does not have a

Manipulation techniques that are less common

Some manipulation techniques are not standard, but have been proven effective when ued. Take a look at some of these:

**Home davantage**

When a person wants to manipulate you, he may insist that you meet in a place where he can easily control you and exert his dominance over you.

They simply take you to their homes, office, car, or any other place where it will be easy for them to maintain their ownership or familiarity becaue you do not have such an advantage.

First, speak to determine your strong and weak points.

It's a common technique with marketers when they're trying to pitch their sales to you. They approach you by asking general probing questions, giving you space to speak for a while. This way, they can determinate your personality, thought pattern, and attitude.

With these findings, they are also able to know your strengths and weaknesses.

This type of manipulation can manifest in your office or your relationships.

**Fact Manipulation**

Lies and excuses are a standard part of this technique. These manipulators are two-faced people. They find ways to blame the victim for being victimized. To accomplish this, they alter the truth or select the information they are willing to divulge. They may also choose not to provide very vital information.

This type of manipulator exaggerates, is biased, and may also be susceptible to understating issues to have things go in their favour.

**Presents Overwhelming Facts and Statistic**

It is a type of "intellectual bullying," and some people enjoy participating in it. This technique entails assuming that they are experts in particular fields or areas of debate. They act as if they know everything there is to know about some places.

However, they manipulate people by providing false facts, statistics, or other data because they know their victims do not know much about the subject. It is a common sales and finance strategy. It's also used in professional terrains and negotiations.

People typically use this technique in social gatherings and other arguments.

Overwhelming Victims with Procedures and Reductions Tape

Some manipulators use officialism, processes, laws/by-laws, organizations, and anyother possible roadblock to exercise their superiority or power while making things harder for others.

It is used to conceal manipulators' flaws and weaknesses, allowing them to avoid scrutiny.

**Raising Their Voices Display of Negative Motions**

To manipulate others in a very aggressive manner, some manipulators raise their voces while conversing with others. They tend to believe that if they can raise their voices and react negatively to things, they will be able to have things their way and have others submit to their wills and get what they want from them.

The over-projection of their voices always comes with some strong body language like pacing or displaying gestures that depict excitement to boost their emotional impact.

**Negative Surprises**

This technique is used to throw people off balance and gain a psychological advantage over them. It occurs more frequently in negotiations. It entails having the victim make assertions that he/she may not be able to follow through on or deliver on in one way or the other.

In most cases, the most potent type of negative surprise occurs without any warnings or signs. The victim is unable to get himself set to count their moves in this manner.

**Making Major Decisions in Limited Time**

It is a common marketing and negotiation strategy. In cases like this, the manipulator pressures the victim into making bad decisions without giving him or her enough time to think it over.

By instilling fear in the victim and gaining control over him or her, the manipulator hopes to weaken the victim's defences so that he or she will eventually succumb to their demands.

**Silent Treatment**

It is a technique in which the manipulator instils anxiety in their victims by making them wait. To achieve their aims, they refuse to pick calls, respond to messages, or attend to their victim's inquiries. The manipulator hopes to accomplish this technique to create a sense of doubt and uncertainty in the victim's mind. That works in their favour because they can sit back and relax in the silence they've created.

Manipulators who use Feigned Ignorance Method by merely acting dumb use this method. They pretend that they don't understand their victims' needs or that they don't know what the victim wants from them. This way, they become both possessive and aggressive, so that you begin to take on their responsibilities and stress over things that you ordinarily should not concern yourself.

# CHAPTER 5

# TYPICAL BEHAVIORS OF MANIPULATORS

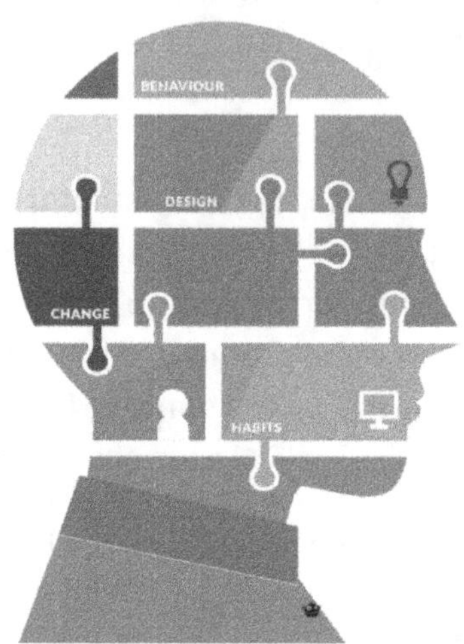


## Handling and Manipulators

Those closest to us do not always want our rights. Friends, relatives, or coworkers can use cancel or reduce self-esteem strategies to cancel or reduce self-esteem strategies to cancel us or reduce self-esteem st These are real manipulation techniques that are frequently ued, for example, by pathologic liars or narcissists.

It is not always easy to accept that you are a victim of these attacks.

However, it is critical to learn to recognize these techniques because they can seriously harm us and increase our insecurities.

However, it must be stated that different levels of psychological manipulation exist, including daily ones that do not seem to cause damage so irreparable or for which it is not always necessary to find oneself on the defensive.

Some forms of manipulation are also used in education and our daily relationships. As a result, it is critical to learn to distinguish between when we are victims of toxic and pathologic behaviour and when we are confronted with forms of daily manipulation that we can learn to manipulate through experience.

## A manipulator's characteristics

There are various types of people who try to manipulate us, often due to insecurities and the desire to "feed" on the confusion or unhappiness of others. Their goal is to make us feel weak, to reduce our self-esteem, and to make us feel guilty for the mistakes they have made.

Recognizing and avoiding these people or their techniques is essential to avoid falling into the hands of these manipulators and suffering the consequences in the long run. Some of the main manipulative techniques are ued here.

### Manipulation Types

Manipulation, from emotional to psychological manipulation, can take hold of different spheres of our being. The pathologic manipulator attempts to identify "buttons," or weaknesses in the victim, to leverage on.

According to Psychologist George K. Simon, for manipulation to be effective, the manipulator must act according to specific rules and behavior and have aptitudes.

- The manipulator conceals his aggression and does not reveal his true intentions. This point is essential for manipulation to well. Typically, two types of masking attack are applied: or through passiveaggressive styles (such as silence or indirect hostility) or types of relational aggression (which include the destruction of the victim's self-e The manipulator can identify the weaknesses of his victims and can create real patterns of manipulation from these weaknesses.

39

- Insensitivity, lack of guilt, and emotional detachment: the manipulator has no qualms about causing harm to his victim if it is useful to his goal.

## Manipulation of the mind

Psychologic manipulation is an interact that results from the exchange between two. And more people, and therefore has a communicative form So, to be a good manipulator, you must also be a great communicator (and the victim must be willing to listen). It is because the concepts expressed by the manipulator, even if simple, leverage the emotional and psychological side of the victim and have a narrative form.

## Motival and psychiatric techniques

Beginning with these considerations, we can try to deepen some emotional and psychological manipulation techniques ued in interpersonal relationships.

## Projecton and Guilt

As we have previously stated, many of these manipulators are insecure and thus "project" their mistakes and shortcomings onto the other person, making them feel guilty. In this manner, the manipulator attempts to turn the situation in his favour.

## Distort Reality

It can happen, for example, dure a date with the partner. The "gaslighting" strategy is used to destabilize and make the other person doubt, and to make them believe that they are living in a fictitious reality. One of the most popular phrases? "It's all the result of your imagination."

## Words Make You Confused

Some manipulators are quite skilled with words. They cage a network of sentences and expressions that confuse and cage the victim. They use original monologues, interrupt the other person, avoid expressing his opinion, and manipulate the conversation. Alternatively, the manipulator can try to buckle words that his interlocutor has never actually spoken, to interpret his thought in a distorted way.

When a narcissist realizes that his techniques aren't having the desired effect, he has two options: insult or remain silent. The victim feels invisible and guilty in the second case. The goal is to humiliate the other person and make them feel bad for not succumbing to their desires and manipulation techniques.

The Fake Good One of the most subtle manipulators is undoubtedly someone who appears to be very friendly and pleasant to the other person but wears a mask. Although you appear to be able to rejoice with the other for the goals achieved, always try subtly to instil doubt or destroy part of the joys conquered.

Lie Manipulators tend to lie very frequently and distort reality, are subtle and appear credible when they speak, and it is difficult to tell if they are telling a

**Omission**

It is a very subtle manipulation modality that consists of not saying and holding back part of the truth, thus modifying all the meaning of the sentence.

**Denial**

The manipulator never admits to doing something wrong, and he always denies any evidence.

**Rationalization**

The manipulator justifies his positions by rationally reasoning them, resorting to a personal interpretation of reality.

**Minimization**

The manipulator tends to reduce the burden of her actions, stating that they are not as harmful as one wishes to believe.

**Seletive attention**

The manipulator focuses his attention only on topics that are of interest to him, implying that he is uninterested in anything else.

**Detour**

When the manipulator does not want to expose himself, he avoids answering questions, diverting the conversation to something else.

**Evasion**

The manipulator provides evasive, irrelevant, and irrelevant answer to the addressed topics.

**Implied Intimidation**

The manipulator uses veiled threats to push the victim to the defensive.

**Insert The Sedan and have FUN**

The manipulator employs sarcasm against the victim, instilling fear and guilt in her until she no longer reacts to situations. These tactics manifested as behaviors such as critical looks, altered tone of voice, repeated and rhetorical criticism, and sarcasm. The victim feels increasingly inadequate to deal with any situation as a result of this tactic.

**Denigration**

It is one of the most dangerous tactics because the manipulator denigrates the victim when she finally begins to defend herself, accuses her of being a manipulator in turn, and tries to go through what she has been subjected to. As a result, the victim tends to withdraw, feeling guilty and sometimes even apologizing to him.

**Feeling Victimization**

The manipulator feels victimized by someone else's circumstances or wishes to elicit pity and compassion from the victim, who is typically a person who tends to take extreme care of those who ask for help and suffer.

**Being available to Simulate**

The manipulator appears to be a person dedicated to a cause of value, pretending to be reliable and available to help those in need.

**Seduction**

The manipulator uses charm, praise, flatters, or openly supports people to lower their defences, gaining their trust and then abusing them.

**Guilt**

The manipulator blames his actions on others, projecting his ideas and intentions onto the victim to whom he ascribes his will. When the victim tries to free himself from the manipulator who will tend to blame her for keeping her tied to himself, he feels that he has done something wrong, that he has pushed the manipulator to say

The manipulator tends to alter reality so that the victim can believe that the vision of the fact that the manipulator proposes is accepted and believed to be accurate. The manipulator even goes so far as to say that the victim deserves to be devalued and accused because she is described as mad when she recognizes manipulative behaviour.

**Simulate being niave**

The manipulator affirms with profound credibility that all his harmful actions are not intental, even feeling indignant and surprised at the accusations made against him. This action aims to make the victim feel guilty for evaluating the manipulator and failing to recognize his good intentions.

**Simulating Perplexity**

The manipulator has no intention of knowing what the victim is talking about. Its attitude confuses the victim, making him doubt his point of view and the veracity of his assertions.

**Anger exhibited**

The manipulator displays ager to frighten the victim and force her to submit. The manipulator is not enraged, but "plays" the role of being upset when he determines what he believes believes believes believes believes believes believes believes believes believes b

**Anger repressed**

It is a psychological manipulation tactic used to avoid confrontation and to tell the truth or to conceal one's intentions. When the victim refuses to adhere to the manipulator's demands, such tactics force the victim to focus on the violent relationship rather than the issue of manipulation.

**Effect of inclusion**

The manipulator tries to trap the victim and force him to submit by claiming that many people have done something similar to what he requires.

Other Mental Manipulation Techniques and that is implemented by the manipulator to weaken the will of the person in front of him As a result, he will be able to shape his mind with various forms of conditioning.

**Isolation**

The human being is a social animal, and a part of the image we have of ourselves that relationships we have. Not only that, but affection, love, communication, and many other aspects are fundamental to the human being. A person who has been isolated from the rest of the world for a long time will begin to have distorted perceptions of reality, allowing his imagination and anxieties to run wild, eventually becoming a victim of his thoughts. Isolation can be a very potent form of weakening and mental persuasion.

**Social Control in Groups and "Group Thinking"**

Solomon Sch, a psychologist, studied group dynamics in-depth to determine how individuals are strongly conditioned in their behaviours and perceptions of what happens. It happens because of what individuals perceive in external reality, but also because of how they define themselves.

For example, if a person in a group labeled in a certain way within the group, they may feel identified with this label over time.

As a result, the group can influence not only how an individual perceives reality, but also how he perceives himself.

## Submission

The manipulation that underlie submission processes are different and compliqued. Still, the central fact is that the manipulator will try to harm the perception of the manipulated person's self to take control of it, making them believe they are wrong or ill. Typically, this type of manipulation creates an addiction, which causes the victim to be unable to get rid of it and to lose sight of reality.

## Exhaustion

Another manipulation tactic is to put the person in exhaustion, attempting to condition and destruct his mind.

Other extreme forms of physical and mental manipulation, such as hypnosis, are used in various contexts. If you feel victimized by spiritual and psychological manipulation at any time, call a specialist who can help you.

# CHAPTER 6

# PSYCHOLOGICAL VIOLENCE IN COUPLES AND FAMILIES

## Signs of emotional manipulation

Emotional maniplation isn't always obvious... Manipulators can be very good at what they do and go unnoticed. So, how do you identify such a situation? Read the text and look for the eight signs of emotional manipulation.

Manipulate by words handler can say things in a genuine and honest way.

They are skilled at concealing their true feelings. For example, you might express anger at them for missing a birthday / special occasion, and they respond with something like, "wow, you make me very sad to think that I would forget your birthday." Or, "Wow, I lie because you make me."

It is common for them to use words to make you feel guilty for something you are not to blame. It can be a small matter of forgetting

46

your birthday and can be a small matter of can be a small matter of can be a small matter of

## Factors that distort

Another type of manipulation occurs when they distort what happened or what you said. Use phrases out of context or retell a fact in their view. And some are so good that they can make you believe it.

They usually justify their bad behaviour and blame you.

They're great at making you feel guilty.

Guilt is a powerful tool for emotional manipulation. It's always you. You either stopped talking or talked too much. You are either overly concerned or do not care. You're either too caring or too sloppy... In any case, the handler will always try to persuade you that it is your fault for the bad behaviour. And they're great at putting themselves in the victim's shoes.

## Reduce Your Problems

Manipulators of emotion don't care about their problems. When you say something like "wow, I have a migraine," they will find a way to convince you that they have a much bigger problem. They will take your lines and make you feel guilty for saying anything because their problems are so much worse, their work is more stressful, and their lives are harder... Or they will try to persuade you of that.

## Passive-Aggressive

In emotional maniplation, passive-aggressive behavior is widespread. They frequently say nice things to you, but they are superficial. Then they will depreciate you, create some problems, and mess up your psychological health. Or they will simply be silenced out of nowhere, making him feel even more guilty and eager to find out what he "did wrong."

Nergetic Vampires and motival manipulators have a dark cloud that follows them wherever they go. When they enter the room, the cloud

47

envelops everyone, so attention fall on them. We feel weakened generally weakened.

They are toxic and will always try to steal our joy. The best thing we can do is walk away.

## Aggression

Handlers frequently use aggressive language and actions to intimidate you. If they realize you will not confront them, they will make you feel uneasy, and therefore they will easily get what they want.

Ggressions tend to get worse and may escalate to abuse as they "advance" in their form of emotional manipulation.

# How do you deal with an emotional manipulator?

### Understand This Person's Need for Acceptance

If the person engaging in manipulative behaviour is a member of the family or someone with whom you believe the relationship should be maintained and helped, try to analyze their attitudes and understand the source. It can be insecurity or a lack of self-esteem. Each of these feelings is a sign of a need, and you can help it by demonstrating that this gap can be filled without depending on, interiorizing, or manipulating others.

It is important to remember that if you want to help, you must stop succumbing to blackmail and attempts at manipulation. Loving entails knowing when to say no and being firm to maintain a healthy relationship, whether it is of love, friendship, work, or family. Dialogue is also a vital thing to seek understanding.

### Seek Understand your Needs and Self-Knowledge

Self-knowledge is the resolution for most of the problems we may have concerning our feelings. A manipulative situation also constitutes a dependence relationship between both parties. If you tend to get carried away by somebody is blackmail, it's because you need acceptance and feel loved, which makes you give into the other's will, even if you don't want to

Knowing your feelings will help you understand why you succumb to manipulation. Through this understanding, you will be able to stand firm and conclude that you do not need to act against your convictions and wishes to be accepted by someone. By demonstrating security over what you want, the manipulative person will see that he no longer has power over you.

**When is it best to walk away?**

There are cases where the best thing to do is move away, preventing the manipulative individual from making you feel ever more dependent and inferior. This attitude is necessary, mainly in abusive-type amorous relationships, in which the other needs to remain in control of the situation and, for this, emotionally and, in the most severe cases,

Breaking a relationship can be very delicate, but in many cases, you need to recover your freedom and individuality. Remember that your happiness and safety must always come first and that it may not be the best choice to make sacrifices just to stay with someone who uses harmful devices like blackmail.

Analyze the relationship as a whole and consider how it usually makes you feel most of the time. That way, you can find the answer to how you shoudle act. And, if you already know what to do, encourage yourself and make your physical and mental well-being and happiness a priority.

Relationships, whether loving or not, should be based on respect for everyone's individualities and desires. You must understand your feelings and desires so that when someone tries to manipulate you, you can identify and lead you to act differently than you think. Watch this out, empower yourself, and take care of your life!

**In relationships, emotional blackmail and manipulation**

## 1. Is the partner amused by your emotions and dismisses them as insignificant?

Manipulators of emotion care exclusively about their feelings and needs. And if you try to start an open and honest conversation with them about those times when you feel underestimated or when it hurts you, your interlocutor will try to "minimize" the conversation as soon as possible. He'll argue that you're acting silly, childish, or, as he puts it, "overreacting" to everything.

Petty Blue, a psychiatrist Hayes claims that "their calm and external rationality, combined with your "inflated" state and sensitivity in such situations, make you doubt yourself and your feelings."

And after a while, you start to wonder if they're right."

An emotional manipulator will never apologize to you for anything...

Instead, he'll blame you for the situation. He'll try to make you doubt your feelings.

So, if you begin to catch yourself on the fact that at the suggestion of a partner, you ask yourself over and over that maybe he's right. And you are really too sensive or take everything too cloe to your heart... This may mean that it is time for you to leave this relationship.

## 2. Is a partner humiliating you?

If a partner consistently insults or laughs at you in public, the likelihood that he or she is an emotional manipulator is very high.

People like this take advantage of your self-doubt to get what they want, but their tactics aren't always obvious. Outwardly, it may appear to your friends and relatives that the partner is merely joking with you and that you do not mind, although you want to scream in pain from a scream.

For example, an emotional manipulator may begin to shame with your friends that you ate three slices of pizza, shaking your head sympathetically and saying something like: "Yes,

According to researchers, many women who were raised in families where their parents constantly humiliated them are used to similar behavior from close Furthermore, they consider it quite normal. As a result, we must draw a clear line between what is permissible and what is not.

## 3. Does the partner absolve you of your bad deeds or bad behaviour?

An emotional manipulator will never accept responsibility for his actions. Instead, he will try to dodge in such a way that he can pin all of the blame on you and prove that his actions were justified. An emotional manipulator always causes his partner to question the veracity of his feelings and the justification of his resentment.

A simple reminder to a partner that he promised to pay utility bills, for example, can cause a flurry of reproaches and accusations in your direction. Like, he ha recently become exhausted at work, that he simply does not have time for all kinds of little things, and that you can do it yourself... And all of this instead of recognizing that he had forgotten about his promise and correcting everything.

## 4. Does the partner refuse to explain his action?

Because they do not want to establish full, real communication with you, emotional manipulators frequently use phrases like "you still won't understand."

They try to assert themselves, to put themselves above you, claiming that their thoughts and feelings are so complex that you can't even fully comprehend them.

As a result, you almost always expect your partner to get anxious because you don't do something you didn't even know about.

**5. Does he try to make himself the most despised and despised person?**

If you tell such a partner that you had a bad day at work, he will immediately begin to convince you that your day was still nothing, but he had a real nightmare. In a nutshell, your feelings again turn out to be depreciated, and you begin to feel guilty for have started talking about your problems.

**6. Partner is "corrected" only when you realize you have enough?**

When you find yourself almost ready to give up and leave a manipulator, they feel as if by some sixth sense.

Just as you're about to say good-bye, your partner transforms into kindness, charm, and courtesy, delighting your hearing with something very similar to an apology... But if you have mercy and forgive him, the relationship is right there, starting to return to the knurled track.

# CHAPTER 7

# IDENTIFYING HIDDEN MANIPULATION

There are various types of manipulation that you will encounter throughout your life. When we talk about covert manipulation, we're talking about the kind that happens beneath the level of your conscious awareness. If you are a victim of this type of manipulation, you will most likely be unaware of what is going on, making it the most difficult type of manipulation to detect and deal with.

Some of the most skilled manipulators will be able to make you doubt your emotional well-being and self-worth, making it easier for them to control you. When you fall into this trap, the manipulator can take away your identity and much of your self-esteem. This takes a long time to complete, but then they have time to get you to do what they want.

Most experts will refer to these skilled manipulators as People who are covertaggressive. They will have a toolbelt of tactics at their disposal to get their target to do their bidding. And, they're usually so good at what they do that the target falls prey without even realizing it. Some of the tactics that a covert manipulator will employ are as follows:

The ability to conceal their disagreeable thoughts.

Make you fearful, make you doubt yourself, and so on, until you are willing to concede or give in to them.


## Manipulators can be dangerous

Emotional manipulators can use almost any type of behaviour to achieve their goals. They are even dangereous when they can read behavioral patterns and the actions of their target. When they can read their target, they will quickly know their target inside and out, such as their level of conscientness, weaknesses, fears, insecurities, and And in the hands of a manipulator, knowledge is power that they can use against their target.

In some cases, the manipulator can even become known as a psychopath. Many manipulators do not fall into this category, but manipulators are really hard to have real relationships with. They will spend a lot of time studying people, and then they will never think twice when they use that information against their target. They are so concerned with getting what they want in every situation that they will not pause to consider their target's feelings or how they should act in a real relationship.

One thing you should keep in mind is that manipulators need to be in control. They are power-hungry, and they will do whatever it takes to achieve that goal. They will frequently injure people in the process, and it will not bother them at all. If you ever feel less superior, less intelligent, less strong, or less confident in your life, especially if you are around a specific person, this person may be

Consider the relationship you're in right now. Are you able to remember when you first met them? Was it magical, something that swept you off your feet? Most manipulators are excellent talkers. They are experts at hiding their real personalities and real plans from their

54

target. They already have plans to trick you into giving them what they want, and they will begin from the moment they meet you.

In the beginning, this person will make you believe that they are willing to do anything for you, and they will continue with this act until you are hooked completely, and you show them your vulnerability.

Once you have done this, they will begin to manipulate you, and sometimes extreme abuse will begin if you allow it.

You will be able to notice that your ideal relationship has changed over time, uually pretty slowly. It has become more perplexing, exploitative, and demeaning. You will notice that the self-esteem you had at the start (whether it was strong or not) will begin to wane, and you will begin to blame yourself for the problem.

At this point, the manipulator will have complete control. It won't be long before you're just getting crumbs out of all the interactions in the relationship. You will be held responsible for everything that goes wrong, even if you had nothing to do with it. You will have to take care of all their needs and care about them all the time, whereas they will no longer care of you or your fears, needs, and emotions. These manipulators do not really care about any of these things; they only pretend to care to hook you on them.

It's incredible how quickly things can change. When a target is under the control of their manipulator, even those with very high selfesteem can turn it around. They will begin to blame themselves for everything that goes wrong in their relationship. They will begin to over-analyze events in their lives, and they will usually do so until they are so confused that they do not know what is going on in their lives. Their mental health, physical health, social relationships, and career can start to suffer because of this confusion and the tactics of the manipulator

The sad part is that the manipulator will be able to do all of this without you knowing where it started. It is not something that happens on a single day and then you can see it and leave. It starts slowly, uually with a few lttle remarks or tactics ued. Then, one day, the manipulator will have taken over all the control, and you will have no idea how to handle the situation or understand what is going on.

# CHAPTER 8

# HOW CAN WE DEFEND OURSELVES FROM ALL THESE PEOPLE?

Psychological manipulation can be quite insidious, easily missed, and have long-term results on one's life. You should always seek to avoid being manipulated by any means necessary. Of course, being able to do this necessitates being able to detect covert manipulation when it occurs so that you can protect yourself as well. Both detection and protection must occur to protect yourself from becoming a victim of manipulation.

## How do we learn to recognize them?

If you remember, cover manipulation is the manipulation of someone that I meant to be hidden. The person being manipulated never be aware of the attempts happening. It is accomplished through a series of actions that degrade self-esteem and self-confidence, leaving the

57

individual exposed and easily swayed. Learning to recognize the following signs of covert manipulation will assist you in protecting yourself in the future. If you are familiar with the characters, you are far more likely to recognize them now than someone with little or no knowledge of manipulation.

**Advantage of home court**

Those who are manipulative tend to seek control in any way they can, and controlling the location for meetings or interactions is one of the easiest ways to get the advantage.

Because the manipulator would then be able to dictate where a discussion occurs, they can be entirely confident with the interaction. In contrast, the other person, who is most likely a target for manipulation, is most likely dissatisfied. It means that a person will already be on edge, distracting from manipulation tactics that can be ued.

**Allowing you to the first speak**

By allowing you to speak, the manipulator can learn things about you and begin determining how best to manipulate you. Consider the salesperson asking you what kind of car you prefer. While you could answer with something as simple as "I want a truck with four doors," or by listing the exact vehicle you want, the salesperson tempts you into answering by asking what kind. You may answer that you are looking for a truck that can be used to haul equipment for your job and have space in the back for car seats for your two children.

You've already given the manipulator valuable information that can be used to steer you into a more expensive car than you might have initially desired. It's all because you were able to speak first.

**Lying or fact-manipulating facts or quotations**

Manipulators frequently lie about facts. They may try to twist facts to benefit themselves in the hopes of keeping you distracted or off-kilter enough that you do not notice or call them out on lying.

They may slightly misquote you in an attempt to use your words against you, or they may twist a phrase that someone influential used to ensure that whatever information is being presented will be beneficial to the manipulator. Consider the adage, "Blood is thicker than water." It is used to express that you owe your loyalty to your family and that blood family is more important than anything else. However, the original quote was, "Blood of the covenant is thicker than water of the womb." The original meaning was that promises made, bonds formed through choice, and oaths sworn were far more critical than blood relatives. It is what manipulators do with their facts: they corrupt what wa said into something that serves their agendas.

**Overwhelming you with stats**

Manipulators, in addition to misquoting or even lying about things, tend to throw massive amounts of knowledge at someone to make them appear more knowledgeable. The manipulator wants to be seen as an authority—one of the ways to persuade others is through appealing to power, what the manipulator wants to do when inundating you Because you are more likely to see someone spouting off vast amounts of useless knowledge about a subject as an authority on that particular topic, you are more likely to allow him or her to do whatever he or she is proposing solely due to your perception of that

**Scapegoating laws or procedures**

Manipulators will seek to use this as reasons for decisions or denials, especially in office settings where there is plenty of bureaucracy. They will apply the paper's rules in any way that benefits them, even if it means cherry-picking which policies and regulations apply to them, but they will hold everyone else accountable. It can cause slowdowns on certain things, such as requesting time off or using vacation hours—they may be allowed to act with discretion but choose not to punish or manipulate others into doing their bidding solely. Those who are willing to follow the manipulator's leads may get that flexiblity, while others are punished with regulations.

**Raising voices or displaying displeasure**

Though manipulators frequently think of themselves as emotionally intelligent and crafty, they are frequently the exact opposite. They struggle to control their own emotions, especially when emotions are high, and may inadvertently explode in anger. They may also use louder voices and aggressive displays of displeasure in ways that encourage people to give in out of fear rather than willingness. They establish themselves as people to be feared by acting almost belligerently, which typically gives them a reputation of being intimidated. People are generally less willing to argue with someone they know is a hothead, even if the declared hothead is incorrect.

**Negative or unwelcome surprises**

Another common tactic used in covert manipulation is to create negative surprises or to present someone unexpectedly to throw people off. For example, if you are going into a negatiation meeting, believe that you and the other company have settled, the other side may install you when you show up to sign the It's meant to knock you off guard because you'll be so caught up in the unexpected, unrealistic suggestion that you'll be distracted.

Furthermore, you have had little time to prepare a counteroffer, meaning you have a massive disadvantage. They may then prey off your unpreparedness, saying that they will need more from you if you want to postpone negotiations again.

**Withholding of time**

It is common in sales positions where you are signing a contract for a big-ticket item, such as a car or a house. The less time you have to debate your decision, the less informed you will be, and the less likely you will think twice about it. If you are told that you have until the end of the business day before a deal expires, and you realize it is 4:45 PM, At that precise moment, you have fifty minutes to decide before your contract expires. You can try to weigh the pros and cons, but ultimately, you will be more easily swayed at the moment than if you have time to reason, make pros/cons charts, or talk the decision through with your spouse to decide if it makes sense for you.

**Arcatic humour**

This type of humour is intended to chip away at your self-esteem. The more worried your self-esteem becomes, the more easily you can be manipulated. Many manipulators will seek to create that low selfesteem by disparang comments hidden behind jokes.

They may make a comment about your last-generation phone, or that you never graduated from college, or even that you chose to eat beef during the work luncheon—after all, didn't Anything that draws attention to you or your choices in a way that diminishes them or implies that they are wrong decisions is a big win for the manipulator, and if you dare get upset, the manipulator will laugh and declare it a joke. You are then left feeling inferior and uneasy in your decisions, doubting your judgment and feelings.

**Making judgments and criticizing yourself or others**

Along with sarcastic humour, but far less covert, manipulators tend to judge others and show no guilt about doing it verbally. They may always identify something incorrectly, but they do not dismiss it as a joke. They may look at your handwriting and declare it is nearly illegible or see a typo in your work and claim you are unprofessional and lazy for not going back to rearn it. Even if you make an effort to arrive at work early in the hopes of impressing this person, you may be told that you are too early and that you should have taken the extra ten minutes to work on all of you, said with a demeaning hand wave at your entire self. Look for people who always have something negative to say to put people down but never provide any real criticism or advantage on fixing the problem— they are probably covert manipulators.

**Playing stupid or incompetent**

The attempt to feign ignorance is one of the most passive-aggressive marks of a covert manipulator. It is done to imply that they do not understand something or are unable to do it competently. Because they cannot do it, the burden of doing so falls on someone else, allowing them to avoid essential duties. Consider how your spouse always gets the dishes wrong. You know your spouse knows how to load a dishwasher—she lived by herself for years before the two of you met, and the dishes were always immaculate when you came to visit. Now, it seems that he can never remember how to load the dishwasher correctly, and you still find dishes with food burnt onto them from the dry cycle, as well as large chunks of food stuck in the trap tha Containers that aren't supposed to be putted through the dishwasher are keept damaged or ruined for one reason. When you try to walk her through how to make the dishes, she nods as if she understands but never changes her method. It tries to trick you into saying things you don't want to say because she doesn't want to.

# CHAPTER 9

# MANIPULATION AND TECHNIQUES USED BY POLITICIANS, THE MEDIA AND SOCIAL MEDIA DANGERS

## Typical salesperson manipulation tactics

Perhaps the most common form of manipulation in today's fast-paced society is the manipulation that salespeople will try and use on us. Most sales tactics rely on basic human emotions such as need or desire, as well as very specific fears such as a fear of missing out or not belonging. Advertisements target us so subtly that we don't realize we're being taken for a ride until we make a purchase we don't need. Advertertisements can play on very primal parts of our brain and get us to do what they want by using fancy colours and enticing cinematics.

Examine the newest advertisements for the iphone and how they show people who are happy while using their fancy brand-new iphone. Are they truly happy becaue of their new iphone, or are they happy becaue of the situations they are shown in?

63

The first step any successful advertisement must take in convincing you that you need it is to convince you that you need it. How can they sell you something if you don't require it? Simply put, they do so by creating these massive social media marketing campaigns in which they show thousands of people queuing up to buy the newest and greatest fancy phone. They can persuade you that if you want to be one of the cool kids, you should also buy into needing something you don't need at all, such as the new iphone.

This manipulation works by exploiting a psychological concept known as "fear of missing out."

Your fear of not keeping up with the curve will entice you to buy the product even if it sets you back financially and even if you don't need it. You may have noticed that the kid's toys in many stores are all colourfully lit and have cool and interesting cut-outs designed to catch the attention of your little tyke. These bright colours and exciting stimuli fire up the reward centers of our brains and prime us to make a purchase.

Another trick that salespeople will try to use is the "fake sale."

You're probably wondering what I mean when I say fake sales. Simply put, if an item has a sticker on it that says it was 15 dollars and is now ten dollars, you'll assume it's on sale and that if you buy it now, you're getting a good deal. Well, the truth is much different than what you think it is - the item is always marked as "on-sale." Salespeople manipulate you on a very primal and basic level, as such it can be hard to avoid and defend against.

Knowing how much something is worth before you buy it is your best defence. Do your homework and research the prices of the item in question, then shop around at different outlets to get a sense of what it is truly worth. This is especially important when purchasing a car, as the stereotypes about used car salespeople exist for a reason. They will tell you whatever you want to know about a vehicle. Their main trick is to quickly get a read on you and learn your likes and dislikes; once they do this, they can trick you into thinking they're your friend. And a friend will always offer you the best deal, right?

This isn't always the case. People who work in this industry do so because they are good people-pleasers - they know what to say to people and how to get what they want from them. You can utlize some of these tricks in your life - the main thing to remember when interacting with someone is to make them feel validated and special. You gain their trust by doing so, and from there you can go far. Feeding into the fact that car sales are mostly a sale. There are also real estate states where a realtor will try to persuade you that something you're going to invest in will only increase in value and you'll be missing out if you don't buy it.

They'll try to entice you with stories about how great the local farmers' market is and how fresh their produce is, or how highly rated the schools in the area are, but the truth is that these are usually just embellishments or outright lies. One thing you may have noticed when looking at potential houses to buy is how the realtor may have baked cookies or prepared candies or cakes. This is done to make you believe that the house is lived in, and it also relies on strong mnemonic cues. Humans strongly associate smells with emotion; as a result, we are quick to dismiss logic, and we will simply go with our heart and ignore the facts.

All manipulation shares the idea of selling us a fake good; the only thing that differs is the end goal.

## Media Manipulation

Now that we've gone over how to deal with manipulation in relationships, I'd like to delve deeply into how the media uses manipulation to get us to buy things or even sway our opinion, and how we can protect ourselves from it.

Consider the mainstream news in the United States. Instead of reporting on just the news and events around the world, certain news outlets will be composed of talking heads and editorials giving their opinion on everything. In a nutshell, they're attempting to persuade you to think the way they want; whether this is due to malice or simple incompetence is debatable.

But the crux of the problem is that when a news story is reported today, it is no longer simply "news" - it is filled with many different people's opinions. And depending on the political leaning of the news outlet, they may not report on other things. Another damaging example of this type of manipulation can be found in social media platforms such as Instagram and Facebook. And that is in the realm of the influencer, someone who is paid to present a false lifestyle and show off how certain products, whatever they may achieve, helped them

This type of manipulation preys on a common psychological trope known as the fear of missing out. When we see these people living super blessed lives and have everything one could want, we start feeling bad about ourselves and, as a result, will The truth is that all salespeople try to persuade us that whatever product they are pitching will make our lives better.

Now that we know this, how can you better equip yourself so that you do not succumb to frivolous purchases of things you do not require? The first step in avoiding this type of manipulation is to take a step back and realize that what people post on social media is what they want you to see. In the same way, what manipulators tell you is what they want you to hear.

With that knowledge, you can better keep yourself from being swayed. The second thing to understand is that if you do decide to buy the products, do research on them, don't just buy something because it has Kylie Jenner's name stamped on it with a bunch of fabulous claims.

Always remember the truism that extraordinary claims necessitate extraordinary facts. You can truly make an informed decision there if you want to purchase something or not. If you've determined that what someone is posting is a pure promotion or that the product is harmful, then and there; you're better off not following it, that will be your final solution if all else fails.

**Advertising Manipulation**

Returning to media manipulation, I'd like to discuss how advertisers try to use the same trick as social media influencers to persuade us to buy things we don't need.

These ads are created in this manner to drive home the point that if you buy these items, you can attain more happiness. This feeds into our desire to be like others as well as our fear of missing out. This type of manipulation is also seen when we go to supermarkets with colourful ads and things that draw our attention from what matters. So your best defence against these forms of manipulation is to research something before purchasing it.

Too often than not, we are persuaded to buy something on an emotional whim and then try to justify it.

**It's possible to be too nice at times.**

This is how we are manipulated; we allow our emotions to override our logic and, as a result, make extremely poor decisions. To defend against this, when shopping or attempting to buy something, always have an idea of what it is you're buying and do not allow yourself to be swayed by mass advertising, as you will be setting yourself up for a whole world of hurt and

Moving on from how salespeople try to manipulate you, I'd like to discuss emotional manipulation and how to defend against it. Some people will try to manipulate you within the confines of a romance, whereas others, such as friends or family, will manipulate you within the confines of an already preexisting relationship. Simply put, it is easier for your friends and family to manipulate you because they do not have the issue of trying to get you into a relationship with them.

Is Your Family Taking Advantage of You?

Relationships are common places to find manipulation, but the most unspoken relationship where manipulation persists is between family members.

Most relatives will not speak up against one another because, because they are related by blood, they emotionally feel that it would be wrong.

Consider the following scenario: your cousin and his two children have asked to move into your home, and you have agreed. After a few months, you notice that he has stopped paying rent, does not buy his groceries or utensils, and instead uses your ingredients and your silverware.

# CHAPTER 10

# WHAT IS PERSUASION?

Individuals will certainly frequently create several solutions when they consider persuasion. Some may consider the commercials, advertisement, and marketing that they see around them that prompt the acquisition of a specific item over a different one.

Others may consider persuasion in regard to national politics, as well as how the candidates might attempt to persuade the citizens' viewpoint to get one more ballot. Both of these are persuasion instances because the message is attempting to transform how the topic is believing. Persuasion can be located in life and it's an extremely effective pressure in addition to a significant impact on the subject and the culture. Marketing, electronic media, lawful choices, and also national politics will certainly be affected by exactly how persuasion functions, and as a result, it will certainly work with convincing the topic.

As can be seen, there are some crucial distinctions between persuasion and the various other types of mind control that we have been gone over in this manual by far. Indoctrination, as well as hypnottherapy, are certainly needed to be based on remaining in seclusion to transform their minds and identification. N adjustment will certainly, additionally serve just a single person to reach the last objective. While persuasion can be did on one by simply conditioning their mind, it is likewise feasible to make use of persuasion on a larger range to convince an entire team and even culture This can make it much more reliable, also potentially unsafe, because it can transform the minds of many individuals at one time, instead of the mind of a solary topic.

Many people fall prey to the mistaken belief that they are immune to the effects of persuasion. They assume that they will certainly have the ability to see any kind of sales pitch that is their way, whether the representative is offering an item or some originality, and after tha This is most likely to hold in some circumstances; no person succumbs to every little thing they listen to in every single moment when they utilize reasoning, particularly if it goes entirely versus their ideas, regardless of

Furthermore, the majority of topics will certainly have the ability to prevent the messages regarding acquiring tvs as well as expensive cars and trucks, or the most recent item on Often, the act of persuasion is far more refined, and it can be harder for them to develop their very own viewpoints regarding what they are being informed.

When the act of persuasion is raised, many people visit it in adverse light. They will certainly consider a salesperson or a conman that is attempting to encourage them to transform every one of their ideas, and that will most likely press and trouble While this is one way to think of persuasion, this procedure can typically be made use of in a favorable means, rather than simply an adverse method. For example, civil service projects can prompt individuals to quit cigarette smoking, or reuse can be types of persuasion that can enhance the lives of the topic. It is simply done by employing the persuasion process.

## Persuasion aspects

When it comes to persuasion, there are specific aspects to be looked out for, just like various other types of mind control. These components aid in specifying precisely what persuasion is, ensuring that it is much more identifiable. According to Perloff in 2003, persuasion is defined as "a symbolic procedure in which interactions attempt to persuade other individuals to transform their mindsets or actions about a concern via the transmission of a

This is just one of the things that distinguish persuasion from the various other types of mind control; the topic is frequently permitted to make their very own cost-free selections in the issue, also if the methods of persuasion The topic can choose which method they wish to believe, if they wish to buy an item or something else, or if they assume the proof behind the persuasion is solid enough to alter their minds.

There are a few aspects that exist in persuasion that also assist in specifying it. These aspects include the following:

- Persuasion is symbolic, which means that it employs noises, photos, and words to ensure that it is understood throughout.

- Persuasion will certainly include the representative intentally trying to affect the subject or team. - Self-persuasion is a crucial component of this procedure. The topic is typically not persuaded, and they are also given the freedom to make their own choices.

- There are several manners that influential messages can be sent, including in-person, net, radio, and TV. The interaction can also take place nonverbally or vocally.

Let's take a closer look at these aspects of persuasion. The first component of persuasion is that it must be symbolic. To encourage someone to assume or act in a particular method, you must be able to reveal to them why they must alter their ideas.

This is most likely to include the use of words, sounds, and images to achieve the brand-new factor throughout. To reveal your factor, you can use words to launch an argument or disagreement.

Photos are a terrific means of revealing the proof that I required to convict a person to go on one means or various others. Some nonverbal cues are possible, but they are unlikely to be as effective as using words and pictures.

The second trick is that persuasion is most likely to be used in a calculated method to affect the means others are acting or believing. This is rather noticeable if you are not deliberately attempt to affect others and are not making use of persuasion to obtain them to alter. The persuader will most likely try a variety of methods to get you to believe similarly to what they do. This can be as simple as having an argument with them or offering proof that sustains their perspective. On the other hand, it can includes a lot more engagement and can even include more deceitful types to transform the topic's mind.

The one-of-a-kind aspect of persuasion is that it allows the subject to have some type of free choice. The topic is able to make their very own fashion selection. In general, regardless of how hard a person tries to persuade them of something, they do not need to go for it. The topic may pay attention to thousand commercials concerning the very best cars and trucks to acquire, but if they do not want that brand name, or are not seeking If the topic promotes abortion, it is unlikely that it will matter to them how many people appear and claim how terrific abortion exactly is. Most likely, the topic will not transform their minds. This allows for a lot more freedom of choice than what has been discovered in the various other types of mind control, which could explain why many people do not see this as a type of mind control when asked.

Persuasion is a type of mind control that can occur in a variety of ways. While indoctrination, hypnotherapy, and control must also take place on a one-on-one basis, persuasion can take place in various other methods. You can discover persuasion instances everywhere, including when you are talking with individuals you recognize, online, and also via radio and TV. It is likewise feasible to give convincing messages in both nonverbal and verbal ways; however, verbal methods are more reliable.

73

# CHAPTER 11

# DIFFERENCE BETWEEN PERSUADING AND MANIPULATION

How does manipulation differ from persuasion? Manipulation serves the person who tries to control someone else's actions or behavior in a way that benefits the manipulator, often through skilful words or techniques, to make the This can be seen in schemes where a lot of convincing, even unethical practices, are used to talk someone into buying something they don't need or making an investment that will help the manipulator benefit, Consider the following characteristics that distinguish manipulation and persuasion:

## Persuasion

There is no intention of taking advantage of someone or duping them into doing something harmful. The reason for persuasion can be benign and thoughtful, frequently putting the other person's interests ahead.

There is no hidden agenda or unmentioned reason for persuasion. The entire procedure is fair and transparent.

The person being persuaded may benefit, or at the very least, the outcome will be neutral or minimal.

As long as the intention is good, there is nothing to hide.

## Manipulation

The intention may involve duping or tricking another person into believing they will receive a reward or other benefit for purchasing or signing up for something, so that the manipulator can profit from the transaction or action.

Manipulation frequently entails concealing certain outcomes or aspects of a decision that could be detrimental, leaving little or no transparency.

Allowing someone to manipulate you into signing a contract for a service you don't need, costing you money you shouldn't spend, while the manipulator stands to benefit from your loss

Because the intention is not altruistic by nature, there is often something to hide or conceal.

A person can be ethically persuaded, because they may already lean in favor of complying with the suggestion or idea that the other person idea. For example, there may be a new vehicle or appliance on the market, and a good friend or colleague may recommend, by way of persuasion, a preferred be They will most likely persuade you because they have a personal and positive experience that they would like to see you benefit from.

On the other hand, a manipulator will try to sell you something less efficient, even damaged, at full charge, and not reveal any deficiencies.

Unless and until their vile methods are discovered, they may be successful in cheating someone and doing so without remorse.

## Keeping yourself safe from abuse

There are techniques you can use in your life to reduce the likelihood of being targeted for abuse and exploitation. It is critical to recognize that not all tactics used are obvious, and some are very subtle, almost undetectable until they worsen over time.

Preventing the impact of abuse may not be easy when the person I cunning in their manipulative techniques. For this reason, it's critical to keep an eye on the early signs that will emerge quickly and occur fairly often in a situation where the goal is to win you over, so that you can be prepared and baited for further control.

The following signs are important to pay attention to because they occur early in a relationship with a person or in the early stages of joining a high control group.

The fact that these early warning signs are easy to detect and similar for individuals as well as groups, should be kept in mind, as they often apply to all forms or tactics used in dark psychology.

**I adore bombing.**

Do you have the impression that someone is too perfect or unlikely to be as good as they appear when you first meet them? They may claim to be your soulmate or express that you are unlike anyone they have met before, or that you are the perfect match for them. This is a common trait in high control groups, where new members are welcomed with open arms and a sudden burst of love and connection is fused, making them feel as they've found the This tactic is known as "love bombing," and it is used to make people feel accepted and valued for who they are. This is a powerful tool for persuading people that they are a part of something greater than themselves, and it instils a sense of duty or obligation, so they simply join and follow the rules without question. In a relationship, the same tactic is used by showing continuous and sometimes extensive flattery and adoration, making a person feel special and loved when in reality, the

## Control over relationships, activities, and thoughts

When you join a cult or a high-control group, you will notice that they have introduced you to a set of rules or guidelines that they expect you to follow without question. They may ask you to spend more time with group members, partake in ceremonies or events, which can fill up your schedule, taking you away from family and friendships that value. They may encourage you to find other people to join and share their message or teachings. The level of control can go as far as dictating personal appearance, thought patterns, and who you can associate with. These are darkerous changes that can affect many aspects of your life. Any disobedience or questioning of their rules can lead to punishment, where other members who have extended their "love" to you are now ignored or treated differently. This will only be restored if you return to your old ways, even if it means losing your own family and friends.

At first, you may see the changes in how you think and associate with people as something positive and energizing. You may believe or buy into their self-improvement ideal and follow them dilligently.

This is where they "sell" you their way of life and persuade you to follow their principles and actions. This is a powerful and deceitful way to gain someone's trust, even if it means instilling fear in them and making them feel incomplete without the group of people involved. You may try to persuade friends and/or family to join an organization or cult because you feel compelled to "save" them, just as other adherents did when they recruited you. Anyone who questions the high control group's teachings, even before joining, may be blacklisted. If you express that family or friends are resistant to get involved, you may be expected to break contact with them. This is where a cult or manipulative group may persuade you that you are better off without family and can thrive with their organization instead, achieving a higher level of existence and satisfaction in life.

77

After becoming involved with a cult of a high control group, your thinking techniques will change significantly. You may have noticed that your level of tolerance is not what it used to be, and you may have adopted some of the manipulative techniques used on yourself to recruit others. Over time, you develop a sense of dependency on them for validation and self-worth, so that any unapproved gestures or comments you make are expediently dealt with through their own conditioning process, either by punishing you with silent treatment or forcing This is a powerful way to keep you under their control while keeping you away from family, friends, and connections.

# CHAPTER 12

# PERSUASION IN MARKETING

It is not as difficult as it appears to get people to say yes to you. You now understand why they decline your proposal, reject your terms, and leave you in a relationship. The line between getting a yes and a no is very thin, but you can improve your chances of acceptance by leveraging the tips here.

**Limitations are being reduced.**

There was a time when I had the opportunity to meet the CEO of one of the best marketing companies. I explained my ideas to him, but he was unimpressed because of how I explained to him. I talked about the idea's success vaguely, using big words that bored him out. However, a colleague of mine pitched the same image to him, and he got an appointment with the CEO. The difference between the two of us was that he explained things in simple terms, whereas I used complicated words. He talked with certainty about the success of the idea, and he was certainty that it wad succeed. The line between getting a yes and a no is very very very very very very very very very ver

The first step in getting a yes from someone is to make what you say appealing to the person's self-concept. It is to say that the person to whom you are speaking must feel involved in what you say. Self-concept has to do with identity, things that can be associated with someone, and the sense of being separated from others. Everyone wants to be treated with importance; whatever you say must appeal to that person's essential things.

Remember the earlier examples of Hopkins and Schlitz. Schlitz purifies his beers in the same way that all other brewers do, but no one has commented on their purity. Hopkins ued this to make his advert, which propelled Schlitz to the top of the chart. He made people believe that his product was the purest and healthiest to drink among all others. In this example, Hopkins knew that people care for their health, which I vital to them.

Those who did not previously drink beer may have begun to do so because the advertisement made it appear healthy.

## Insurance Companies' Lessons

Because their insurance policies appeal to their self-concept, insurance companies have a large number of customers. Many people want their properties to be safe. So they don't mind paying what appears to be stipends to ensure that. Insurance companies have policies in place to ensure that their customers feel secure about their properties.

A car policy, for example, is one of the ways insurance companies persuade their customers to insure their cars with them. They provide systems such as "if your car gets stolen or damaged, giving you have paid certain beneficiary sums, we will get you a new car or fix the damage without any expenditure accru You can see that that is a tempting offer, and many people will want to jump at it because it appeals to their interest, which has to do with securing their properties.

There was a time at my workplace when some insurance agents came to advertise their policies. It was a health insurance policy. They offered to pay for the health services any worker would need if they ever fell sick for a little over peanuts in our annual income. Even though I no longer work for the company, I continue to use the policy, as did many others when it was implemented. Their offer was able to persuade us to accept their system because it appealed to our interest.

It means that if you want to persuade someone to listen to you and accept your opinions, you must consider what you can do to appeal to their self-interest. Create messages or instances dedicated to them. Instead of bragging about how great your idea is, tell them how it will benefit them. For example, if you want to get a job or a promotion, you must demonstrate what you stand to gain if you are given that position. Create marketing messages dedicated to prospective clients if you want to gain more customers as a businessman. The letters should not discuss the company, but rather how the products can benefit them.

Cue from movie and game makers Game and movie makers seldom talk about how good and powerful they are. On the other hand, they rarely talk about the educational qualifications and capability of their workers. Instead, they talk about their products, features, and how they can add value to the lives of their customers.

Furthermore, most game enthusiasts watched the youtube video session of the new PS5 that would be released very soon. There were great comments after the video session, and many people would buy the console. Why? It's very simple. Sony didn't just show customers that they could make video game consoles or hire the best software engineers for their products.

Instead, they informed their customers that the new product would provide them with a more natural gaming experience. The company also informed buyers that they could play certain X-Box games with the console, among other things. Sony not only demonstrated that they had created another product, but it also demonstrated to customers the benefits of purchasing their latest game console.

More so, before vengers nd Game was released last year, many already buyed tickets of cinemas that ware showing it. Why? It's exactly like what I explained earlier. They created awareness that appealed to the target audience's interest in watching a fantasy movie of superheroes.

So, to get desired responses, you must have something that appeals to your audience's interest. It would get you that promotion, the respect and appreciation you desire from your children, and the sales you desire. It will help you achieve your goals. If you can't make your proposal appeal to the interest of the person to whom you're presenting it, you'll never be able to persuade that person.

**Always offer Value**

If you want to win over someone and sweep them off their feet, you must make them believe that whatever you are offering them is worthwhile.

Top brands understand that offering value is the most practical and sustainable marketing strategy. When you buy a high-quality product, you will tell your loved ones to do the same. Referrals will go a long way toward establishing a product's authenticity and constructing a company's image. Social media make spreading the news eay.

Nike, for example, endores celebrities to help the appeal of her products. However, its high customer satisfaction is not based on this approach. The company provides some of the best quality shoes in the world. Nike develops its footwear with good texture. Aside from that, the interior is very soft, which provides comfort to the feet and allows you to move around easily while wearing it. So, the success of this organization is based first and foremost on quality products and, secondarily, adverts.

People use the same model. When it releaed its latest product, iphone 11, it made the features appealing to customers.

Regardless, the vast sales were about the phone's exciting parts as well as its impressive marketing strategies. For example, the nature of this new product's security makes it appeal to top people in the business world. Individuals like these can rest assured that their data is secure on this phone.

Over seventy-five percent of mericans lament that they made an impulsive purchase. In other words, they purchased items they had never desired or planned to purchase. This is known as Post Purchase Cognitive Dissonance. They will believe that the purchase was not worthwhile. It has been ingrained in their minds that they will not invest in similar products based on their past experiences. So, to persuade them to buy your product, you must get your promotion right. Nevertheless, beyond the advert, you must be able to offer them product that prove them value.

# CHAPTER 13

## HOW WE ARE PERSUADED TO BUY WHAT WE DON'T NEED

Persuading people is the last part of the three-step process for successfully manipulating someone. After you've planned the manipulation seeds, you'll want to use persuasion. Manipulation is where you offer the solution, and persuasion is where you get to tip them over the scale so they say yes. Manipulation primarily relies on verbal techniques, whereas persuasion is a series of verbal and physical techniques that you use to really get the person on your side and

## Overcome their trust problems

People will always have trust issues. One of the best ways to persuade someone is to learn how to overcome someone's trust issues so that they trust you. While this can take weeks or even years for some people, master manipulators are great at earning trust in a matter of seconds. It works by being charismatic, remaining confident, and retaining authority in your conversation. When you are able to lead the conversation, be friendly and open to the person you are talking to, and really get them to warm up to you, it becomes a lot easier for you to per This is the very first part of persuasion that you should practice every single time, no matter what drives them, what the solution is, or what you want to gain from the experience.

## Understand your product (or purpose).

When attempting to manipulate people, you will have to overcome objections. They'll ask questions, have concerns, and want to make sure you're not just trying to pull their leg. Even if you are, you mustn't appear to be. Having a clear understanding of your product or purpose is a great way to ensure that you can provide answers and explanations for any objections in a second, without missing a beat.

When you have to stop and think about why someone should agree with you, you ultimately give them several minutes to think about why they should not agree with you. The faster you respond with your reasoning, the more likely they are to agree with you. This demonstrates that you are educated, have a purpose, and know everything that I needed about either the product or the purpose behind what you are asking for.

Here are an example of a conversation where you overcome the object                                                              by knowledgengengengengengengengengengengengengengengengengeng engengengengengengeng Assume you're trying to find someone to cover your shift because you don't feel like going to work that day. If you simply state that you do not feel like showing up, they are unlikely to cover your

85

shift. However, if you have a good reason for not being able to attend, they are more likely to make it work. Here's an example of the conversation:

"Hello Peter, can you cover my shift today, please?"

"I don't know, but I'm busy today," Peter says.

"But my car broke down, and I don't have a way to work," you say.

"Can't you take the bus?" Peter asks.

"One does not run past my house, and I do not have money for a taxi." I really need my shift covered, though, so that our boss doesn't get anxious with me; I had to miss a shift last week as well for a doctor's appointment."

"That stinks," Peter says. But I'm not sure."

"Please, it's only a 9-12 shift, so you won't be there long."

Catherine is already doing the majority of the work, so all you have to do is show up for the three hours and get paid."

"I believe so," Peter says.

"It's basically like getting paid to sit there, and I know you asked the boss for extra shifts last week." "Are you willing to take it?"

"Okay, fine," says Peter.

Here, you gathered evidence and explained why Peter needed to cover your shift. You not only appealed to your need, but you also appealed to his need. Finally, you want to make your offer sound like they need it more than you need them to take it.

When you can make it sound like it's good for them, the person you're trying to persuade is far more likely to agree.

**Keep a calm and confident demeanour.**

In addition to being able to appeal to someone who is needed to trust you, and to being charismatic and authoritative in a conversation, you need to know how to stay calm and confident. There will be times when you feel nervous or like you want to break character and express emotions other than calmness and confidence. If you do, however, you will not be able to persuade people. Instead, emanate calmness and confidence the entire time.

When people begin to object to what you are asking, remain calm and confident. Ssert why they are needy and stay potive in your position. Do not get desperate or push for them to agree with you or side with you. Instead, remain calm and confident as you progress through the various stages of manipulation. At some point, you will gain their trust and they will follow you. If you break character, they may begin to see through your actions and realize that you are only trying to manipulate them and that you aren't actually paying attention to their

This is also true during the conversation's informative portions.

When they ask you a question, give them answer with clarity and confidence. Be very assertive about why they need what you are offering, and never waiver. When they ask about a certain feature, explain what that feature does with complete confidence, even if you aren't completely sure you understand it yourself.

The more confident you are, the easier it is for you to keep people confident in you and what you are talking about. Then they will be more likely to agree with you and accept what you are offering.


**Manipulate your body language.**

As you are aware, body language is massive. Most of us can read it as a basic survival skill. However, many people do not realize they are reading it. Furthermore, some will realize they are reading your body language and maybe well-versed in what different signals mean. You need to manipulate your body language to comply with what you are trying to accomplish for both reasons. For example, if you are trying to sell something and want to be confident, you cannot be expressing nervous body language. This will cause people to wonder what you're trying to hide and will cause them to distrust you or your offer. Alternatively, if you are feeling desperate for their compliance and show this through your body language, they are going to see your desperate and believe that you are not genuinely trying to help

When working to manipulate people, always ue confident body language. The only exception to this rule would be if you were playing the victim. Then, you must use body language that makes it appear as if you are being attacked or otherwise threatened by the person you are attempting to manipulate. In general, you want to stand with a tall posture, broad hears, and your head parallel to the flood. Do not turn your nose up at people, and do not look up at them by turning your head downward. Instead, attack them straight on, smile, and make sure to practice so that you can respond without missing a beat.

# CHAPTER 14

# DIGITAL NATIVES

We live in a world where many of its inhabitants are considered digital natives. This is an era where connecting with a mass audience has become as easy as here and there.

Although connectivity has become more of a friend than a foe, it has also become more difficult to persuade or influence a larger audience. Getting to the very core of influencing has become more difficult as we now live in a world where we are bombarded with digital information on all sides.

## Increasing your influence at work in this digital age

A glance at the Dale Carnegie Training When the term 'INFLUENCE' I mentioned, the name Dale Carnegie I mentioned and the name Dale Carnegie I Dale Carnegie Training has produced several leaders, presidents, and top business tycoons such as Lee Iacocca and Warren Buffet. Dale Carnegie's has also been revised to be suitable to today's era and has been aptly called 'How to Winning Friends in the Digital ge'.

This emphasizes a very important message – that the value of human communication is now often utlized to achieve transactional facility. Furthermore, it emphasizes a significant disadvantage of using digital communication heavily to influence people, and that is building trust through human and direct communication.

## Avoid Arguments

Avoid arguments as much as possible. To truly influence people, you must understand that persuading them does not necessitate arguing with them. Ask yourself, "How will that person trust me if I constantly provoke him or her?" Saying aloud that the person is 'wrong' will not help the discussion.

The truth is that arguing will not get you anywhere. Worse, it only results in the other person being adamant about how correct he or she is. Even if you are completely correct on one point, arguing makes you appear futile and ineffective.

Leaders must be able to disagree with their followers in the most tactful way possible. If you want to influence your subordinate, you must know how to draw the line between a tactful discussion and a heated argument.

Participating in deferential negotiation I even more considered effective in the long run.

## When you're wrong, admit it.

OK, this may hurt your pride, but you will lose all of your influencing power if you do not immediately admit your own mistakes. It is quite normal for people in positions of power to admit their mistakes. However, if you are able to readily admit that you made a mistake, you are communicating a positive message to people – that you genuinely care for them and that your behavior

Another benefit of being able to admit when you're wrong quickly is that it protects you from negative news and gossip.

Remember that a small matter can turn into a colossal matter when the gossip hyenas begin to spread them around. So, as this demonstrates, come clean immediately.


## No credit gabble

So you want everyone to recognize you as a great leader.

However, this does not imply that you are entitled to every credit that goes to your team. Quality leader NVR grabs the credit that really below the members. If you constantly fantasize about being in the spotlight, don't expect your team to respect, follow, or simply listen to you. No, you will not be able to influence them or gain their trust.

When you allow other people to shine, you will be able to convey the message that you appreciate their efforts. If they believe this, they will be motivated to work harder and put in more effort for you and the team. This will make it easier for you to persuade them to do their best all the time.


## Make an effort to be personable.

There are times when you may want to share a few details about your personal life at work. People will be able to see the 'human side' of you by opening a small window to your life outside the four corners of the office. This helps especially when interacting with your colleagues is difficult to do regularly.

Being personable removes the barrier between you and your colleagues. It makes you less intimidating and allows people to see the authentic you. When you draw or create a connection between yourself and others, you can strengthen your professional relationships as well.

**Increasing your social media influence**

One aspect that we must all learn is how to increase our influence on social media. The ubiquity of social media platforms is unavoidable these days, and being able to use it effectively can also help you become an individual of influence.

Your social media presence is the fundamental foundation of your influence, and you must capitalize on it. To begin with, creating and managing accounts can aid in the creation of a large footprint. It is important to note that seeing your name or stories on the newsfeed, or starting your following, does not necessarily mean you are already an influencer. It takes more than that to be a person of influence on the virtual platforms.

It's worth noting that influencers and their followers form a strong bond while earning through conversions. People are interested in what you have to say and are excited to hear what you have to say. If you want to learn more about how to become a person of influence on your favorite social media platform, then go ahead and apply these tips.

**Provide your followers with mind-blowing content at all times.**

The WOW factor is what keeps followers interested. Never waste your time on content that would eventually be a waste of space. Mediocrity has no place in the online world. Posts that are sloppy and irrelevant will simply wash your influence away. Only share posts that are well-written, helpful, and insightful to become a person of influence. Give your followers something to chew on after reading your post, while leaving them hungry for another.

**Always share data that is logical and backed up with opinions.**

Being able to express your opinion and make predictions can make a person influential as well. Never be afraid to use infographics, graphs, and other statistics to convey your message.

As mentioned in the first tip, being insightful is a great tool for making your presence felt and your voice heard in the realm of social media.

### Initiate connections and conversations with your followers.

Being able to initiate trending conversations is extremely beneficial. By initiating these conversations, you can expand your network and increase your following. For example, if you want to do a Q&A with your followers, you can do so and create an eye-catching hashtag to go with it. Many others would start searching for your conversations that way.

### Keep track of your presence.

To see if your influence has gotten a notch harder, keep tabs on yourself. For example, you can begin measuring how people perceive you online. You can do this by creating Google lerts for yourself and your business.

### As much as possible, avoid drama.

The fact that influencers are not afraid to speak their minds does not necessarily mean that you can engage yourself in all sorts of topics or discussions. Try to avoid drama as much as possible, but do not shy away from any controversy. Feel free to express your strong opinions on topics related to politics and social issues. Do not be afraid to engage other known individuals also.

### Develop strong relationships with other social media influencers.

When it comes to building a strong online presence, networking is a must-have tool. Your followers would love to see how you are related to certain personalities. If you're just getting started, you could contact these people and see if you can be of any assistance to them. You'd see the benefit of doing these in the long run.

**Ttend to have your presence felt in their places.**

If you spend all of your time on social media, you're missing out on one crucial tool that could help you grow your influence quickly. Yes, try to make a name for yourself in other industries as well. Write for various industry publications to expand your business. Make some meetups so that you can meet your followers in presence as well. You'll be surprised at how quickly your presence can grow once these people start talking about you.

**Boost your personal branding**

You'd find that influencers have a great personal branding.

BY creating a persona and maintaining a voice online, you will become more recognizable. For example, have a key phrase that you would constantly use in your post.

You will be able to help people remember your content and even your name if you do this.

**Never feel afraid to speak about your accomplishment.**

To be a person of influence, you must first be a person of substance. And how do you persuade people that you are?

You would be able to make them look at you as a leader by speaking about your accomplishments and qualifications. Wards, products launched, number of speeches given – all of these can be ued to gain online influence.

**You can also get personal.**

People may not need to know about your divorce, bankruptcy, or solo parentship. Sharing these, however, may help them realize that you are also someone like them — wth imperfect, failures, etc. When your story resonates with them, you become a more interesting person, and people want to follow you around.

Once you've begun to be an influencer, you'll need to learn how to sustain and further boost it.

# CHAPTER 15

# THE PRINCIPLES OF PERSUASION

To master the art of persuasion, you must be aware of the underlying principles that will enable you to harness your influence. In general, human beings are a touchy lot; one wrong move and you'll lose all ability to persuade people to join your team. You must make strategic decisions that are guided by the necessary fundamental principles. The six principles of persuasion are reciprocity, consistency, social evidence, liking, authority, and scarcity.

## The principle of reciprocity

Reciprocity is simply doing to others what you would have them do to you.

Reciprocity calls for respect and kindness as you go about your everyday experiences. It is a good thing to be kind to others because it makes others feel better about your intentions. If you have been very nice and kind to someone else, you have a better chance that they will be nice and kind to you.

If you want to persuade someone, you must behave towards them in a decent manner. Speak a word of kindness to them, do them a favour, or even buy them a gift. After all, you've proven yourself to be a kind human being who cares about him.

In persuasion, the cohesion principle of Consistency works as follows: People are more likely to commit to larger tasks or favours once you have persuaded them to agree to smaller ones. That is, if you can get them to spring a puddle for you, you can get someone to swim oceans for you. A few studies have been conducted to support this hypothesis. For example, in one study, a group of researchers asked some homeowners to erect a hideous Drive Safely billboard on their front lawn. A few homeowners declared yes. The researchers, however, had to take a diferent approach to the experiment: first, they got homeowners to agree to the small commitment of putting up a Drive Safely posts Despite its lack of aesthetic appeal, more homeowners agreed to put up the billboard this time. The reason for this is that the homeowners subconsciously felt compelled to maintain their earlier reaction.

The technique of foot-in-the-door compliance relies on consistency. It means getting people to consent to a larger request by first checking the waters with smaller requests. If you want to execute this strategy cleverly, your target will need to be trained to be consistent with their responses to your qestion.

For example, if you want your employee to work the weekend shift, you might want to get them to agree to work the overnight shift — or vice versa, depending on which shift in your business is the least preferred one.

## The principle of liking

If a person likes you, they are more likely to fulfil your demands, no matter what that may be. A person who is disliked and also dislikeable will hear no more times than a well-liked person.

97

But how do you get people to like you? According to science, the secret to being loved is a combination of three main factors.

First, people prefer those who are close to them. You must find common ground with them to look closely at the person you are attempting to persuade. For example, many foreigners have learned that learning and speaking the local language I the mot eay way to become more likable. Another thing to keep in mind when making yourself more likable is flattery. If you use it correctly, Flattery will open many doors for you.

Citizens prefer those who pay attention to them. If you want to ask someone to do something for you, start by giving them a genuine compliment first. Just because it's called flattery doesn't mean you have to be effusive about it. Excessiveness in your praise will be counterproductive to your desire to be liked. Finally, be the type of person who is usually pleasant and cooperative in achieving mutual goals, and you will be one step closer to being pleasant. If you're always stepping on the toes of others to get what you want, you'll have very few friends, which won't help your case when you need to convict someone in the future. Remember that being pleasant and cooperative does not imply being a doormat. Sometimes it simply means putting in a little effort to assist someone in achieving a goal that is important to them. For example, if a colleague is struggling with a due report, offer to assist them with the printing and mailing process. It's not a lot of work, but you'll go from being an uninvolved, unwritten colleague to a kind and helpful colleague.

## The authority theory

When compared to a complete newbie, a person who is an authority figure in a particular field will have an easier time influencing others.

If you want to persuade more people to do something specific, you need to build your credibility by making yourself seem as you have expertise in whatever field you play. This is a key reason why professionals in their field display their diplomas. Consider this: if you walked into a therapist's office, you would most likely deliberately look for the kind of qualifications they have hung on their walls. If your therapist has a lot of credentials displayed in this way, you will probably feel a sense of comfort in their experience. As a result, you will quickly accept and follow any advice they have for you. Ssentially, the therapist has managed to manage to manage to manage to manage to manage to manage to manage to manage

It's a fact that if you're the only one talking about it, your authority won't be taken seriously. As a result, you must ensure, so to speak, that you recruit others to beat the drums on your behalf.

There are subtle ways to accomplish this. You can identify a field in the office that you are passionate about and become that field's office guru. For some, this could be Microsoft xcel or Reporting. The man known as the xcel office guru will have a much easier time getting things out of people because they already know what he is talking about. He has also proven to be likable and helpful by resolving all their problems with xcel, and his colleagues may want to pay him back in some way. To make your mark around the world, you do not need to learn xcel. There are many other fields where you can excel and present yourself as a figure of authority.

## The Scarcity Principle

In economics, the laws of demand and supply are straightforward: when supply is low and demand is high, prices rise. To put it another way, the value of scarcity rises. If you are a businessperson who wants to persuade people to buy your product or service, it helps to highlight the fact that the product is on offer for a limited time. Furthermore, inform customers that if they do not obtain this product on time, they will suffer significant losses.

If the marketing message is packaged in this manner, more people will rush to beat the time limit on your product.

It is critical to becoming a scarce product for yourself in the world of business and personal relationships. If you are not available to others when they require you, you will quickly lose your value. If you want to keep your aura of mystery and power around you, you must learn the art of being inaccessible and unavailable. When you appear, your word will be respected more than a person's word that appears and speaks of all importance and meaning.

## The consensus theory

People look at others who are like them in everyday interactions for clues as to what to do or say. A good influencer understands that all it takes is one person to buy into their idea, and the rest of the crowd follows suit. There are various ways you can apply the consensus principle to your benefit. Because their peers have said so, these colleagues are more likely to be convinced of the worthy cause.

Why do you believe this, and how does this segment affect you as a buyer? You will most likely consider purchasing these other items because they were purchased by customers with similar tastes and needs to yours. You may not have intended to purchase the additional items, but the fact that it was done by others will lead you to believe that you do. In effect, this is the principle of consensus.